AGING PARENTS

AGING PARENTS
When Mom and Dad
Can't Live Alone Anymore

Eldon Weisheit

A LION BOOK

Copyright © 1994 Eldon Weisheit

Lion Publishing
20 Lincoln Avenue, Elgin, IL 60120
ISBN 0 7459 2625 8

Cover by Walljasper Design

First edition 1994

Libray of Congress CIP Data Applied for

Printed and bound in the USA

Contents

——Preface——
How to Get Your Money's Worth out of This Book

This book is for adult children who must make decisions regarding housing and physical care for parents who cannot make the decisions themselves. It's for you when your mom and dad can't live alone anymore.

Although this book speaks specifically about caring for aging parents, its message applies to everyone who must make decisions for elderly or handicapped people who can't take care of themselves. Too often people make decisions and ask questions later. The purpose of this book is to help you ask the questions first—so the decisions you make will be as informed as possible. Hopefully, it will you will help you to avoid three common mistakes.

Missing the big picture. Some people look at only one part of the problem and make their decision based on that single issue. Later they become aware of many other factors they should have considered. Then they face a double problem: Correcting the old decision and starting over again.

Overlooking all of the facts. Some people collect only a few facts before they make their decision. Their own emotional involvement, their anxiety about helping their loved ones, and their lack of experience sometimes prevent them from seeing all of the needs. You need to take the time to look at all of the options that are available for your parents.

This book shares the experiences of hundreds of people as they faced the same issues that you face now. Some may not apply to you—at least, not yet. But scanning those parts will give you a broader picture of the dilemmas many families face.

Hoping for perfection. Finally, some people search so long for information that they never get around to acting on that information. It is tempting to put off making a decision that is difficult and will affect many people. But there is a time to think, and a time to decide. This book will help you as you work through the thinking process, so you can make the best decisions. Although you will never be sure that you are 100 percent right, you can know that you have done your best for your parents under the circumstances.

This book is not like the old arithmetic texts that had the answers in the back of the book. My purpose is not to make a decision for you, but to guide you through the decision-making process. Many of the facts that you need will vary from time to time and place to place; for example, I cannot give the dollar- and-cent cost of care in facilities for elderly people in your area. But I will give you suggestions on how you can collect that information, and how you can find additional agencies in the community that offer special services for the aged.

Along the way, I want to share with you the experiences of many other people, so you can benefit both from their mistakes and their successes. Experience is indeed the best teacher, but if you must experience everything for yourself;

then it is also the most expensive teacher. Learn from the experiences of others and you get the lesson without paying the tuition.

The stories in this book come from my thirty-something years as a clergyman, from responses to a questionnaire that I sent out as I worked on the manuscript (see Appendix 1), and from my personal life. Some of the stories may seem extreme to you—either extremely naive and too-good-to-be-true or extremely difficult and nobody-has-it-that-bad. But that's why these stories are so important. The demonstrate the wide range of experiences people have as they deal with the issue of carrying for their loved ones. If you identify with all the good stories, thank God for your blessings and strive to be helpful and understanding with others in your situation who don't have it so easy. If you identify with the tragic stories, take comfort in knowing that you are not alone, and don't be afraid to ask for help. Of course, you will probably find a little bit of your family in most of the examples.

Many of the stories have been edited to make them apply to more situations. Some of the stories have been combined with others because there are many recurring themes that happen among elderly people and those who work with them. Most often names have been changed to prevent any unnecessary invasions of privacy.

Notice also that this is written about the care of parents as though you are making a decision for both your mother and father at the same time. In a few cases that will be true. In more situations the reader will be concerned about either a mother or a father. I trust you to translate my plural "parents" (easier to handle than a constant list of "he or she") to the person or persons depending on you now.

I thank all the people who responded to my questionnaire, to those who have told me their stories, to the old people who have richly blessed my life, and to the people who work in the facilities for elderly people that I visit regularly. All of them have contributed to this book and have allowed me to use their lives to help others. And a special thanks to the many senior citizens of Fountain of Life Lutheran Church in Tucson, Arizona, who have given me a good example of how to grow old with a flair.

—Eldon Weisheit

——Prologue——
Welcome to the World
of Old People

All of us live in a community made up of many smaller sub-communities. Because you are a part of some of those sub- communities, you probably don't pay much attention to them. They are part of your everyday experience. However, there are also little communities in the bigger world of your neighborhood that you may not be aware of—or which you may know about but rarely see.

One of those sub-communities is the world of small children. Unless you have a little one in your family, or have another connection with a child, you may rarely see it. But the world of small children is there in nurseries, day-care centers, pre-schools, playgrounds, pediatricians, the tooth fairy, Sunday school, swimming lessons, baby sitters, pets, and a variety of other places and things that provide the stage for a child's life.

There is also a world of old people in your community. Do you already know about it? If not, the fact that you have chosen to read this book means you will soon discover it. It is a world of nursing homes, retirement communities, hearing aids and canes, grandchildren, Medicare, senior-citizen discounts, long vacations, medications, and special diets.

People have different views of the world of old people. Some try to pretend it is just this side of the Beautiful Isle of Somewhere. They call old age the golden years of life. They would be offended by the term old people; people are "chronologically gifted"—not "old." The residents of this special world don't have to work. They sleep late every day. They cash checks that come to them from previous jobs or investments. They travel and enjoy sports, theater, and dances every Friday night. They play golf and sit by a swimming pool.

Such a view is for people who live in a pretend world. The real world of old people is not a perfect place.

Others see the world of old people as not far from hell itself. It is the place for people with bodies but not minds, a place for wheelchairs and hospital beds. It is where people can't enjoy food or the company of other people. It smells of urine and sounds of people saying the same non-sensical thing over and over. It is a world with no memories of yesterday and no hopes for tomorrow. This view, too, does not describe the real world of old people.

The world of old people is as varied as the community in which it exists. Some of its citizens are happy and content, and others are miserable and grouchy. It has people who laugh and tell jokes, and it has people who cry and ask for help. It includes sweet little grandmothers and bitter old ladies, kindly grandfathers and dirty old men. It is a real world.

This is not a book of statistics, but you need to know a few of the figures at the outset. The fastest growing age segment in America is the sixty-five and older group. The majority of middle-aged people now have more parents than they have children. Those who are sixty-five years old have a forty percent chance of needing to live in some type of long-term care health facility. Sixty percent of those who are seventy-five will need such care. About ninety percent of those who enter a nursing home will be bankrupt if they must pay their own expenses for longer than two years.

Your ability to help your parents in the world of old people depends upon your ability to treat them as real. If you deny their problems and pretend that age has not changed them, you will not be able to help them. Likewise, if you regard old age as an illness from which they will never recover, you will be of no help to them. To be a help, you simply must be willing to assist them in their problems and share in their joys.

You may want to avoid dealing with the reality of old age. If so, let me point out two simple facts to you. The people you love will become old. Will you stop loving them because of their age? Is there a time, a certain birthday, a certain physical or mental handicapped that will be a termination notice to your relationship? I hope not. You would be the loser in the relationship.

The second fact: If you are fortunate, you will someday be a part of the world of old people. Explore the world now so that it is not foreign to you when you become a citizen there. Learn how to enjoy the age you are now. Too many people spend the first half of their lives wishing they were older and the last half wishing they were younger. Learn to live in—and enjoy—the present.

For now, you may be a visitor to the world of old age. Someday you will be a resident. Look forward to it.

——— 1 ———
The Tables Are
Turned—on You

For some people it happens in a moment. The message comes via a phone call or a letter.

Dad fell off the ladder. His hip is broken — a bad break. The doctor says it will heal in time, but that Dad will not be able to live by himself anymore. He told us to start looking for a place where Dad can have round-the-clock care.

Mom had a stroke yesterday. We were scared. Sorry I didn't have time to call you then, but I felt I had to stay with her in case she didn't make it. The doctor says that she will pull through, but he says she will never fully recover. We have to think about what will happen when she leaves the hospital.

Suddenly you have a responsibility that you may not be prepared to accept. You may not even be sure what questions to ask. And you may be even less sure about who has the answers.

For others, change is a gradual experience. They see their parents slowly show signs of age. Those who live away from their parents are shocked at Christmas or vacation time when the family is together—"Mom looks so small" or "Dad seemed to have forgotten who I was. I think he mistook me for Uncle Ralph."

Those who see their aging parents on a daily basis often do not see, or choose to ignore, the signs of physical and mental deterioration. Then suddenly the change is obvious.

I was singing in the church choir and noticed a little old lady in the third pew. Then I realized she was my mother. But it couldn't be! I had seen her every week and had not noticed that she had grown old. My mother is energetic and full of life. The woman in the pew looked empty—as though her life had already left her body. I realized that I had to face reality. I was living in the past by pretending my mother was who she used to be. I had to look to her future.

However the message is delivered, and no matter how long you try to avoid hearing it, the truth will finally come through. The tables have been turned. Your parents, who made decisions for you for many years of your life, must now depend on you to make decisions for them. You, by yourself or with others, must decide where your parents will live, who will provide for their care, who will see that they receive proper medical care, and who will handle their finances. This list of decisions that must be made is not an easy check-off list for one person to do—or to be divided among those who share the responsibility. Each decision is related to and a part of the others. They truly are family decisions.

1 • The Tables are Turned–on You

Panic and Guilt

It is natural to panic, to jump to instant (and negative) conclusions. "I can't have my parent live with me." "I can't afford to pay for a nursing home." "I don't have time to visit them every day (week, month)." "My spouse (or children) has to come first." All of those thoughts are necessary. And just as they may be true, they may also be adjustable. You will come to a better decision if you start with what is possible, rather than that which is not possible. If an instant decision must be made about where Mom and Dad spend next week, take what is available and recognize that it is a temporary solution. Then, when you have some breathing space, take time to evaluate the needs and possibilities of a long-range decision.

> I panicked when I realized my parents could no longer live alone, because they had different needs. Mom could have easily lived with me. No problem. But Dad had to be in a nursing home. I had always seen them as a pair; there was no way that I could think of them living in different places. So I felt there was no possible solution to my problem.

Guilt is another reaction to the awareness that your parents can no longer live alone—for some, make that GUILT (Industrial Strength). You may feel guilty about past family problems. You may feel guilty because you didn't recognize your parents' problems sooner. You may feel guilty because you think you cannot provide the care they need.

Like panic, guilt is a negative motivator. Starting with a sense of guilt will cripple your ability to help your parents. Or guilt may make you overcompensate, causing you to help your parents while ignoring other family members. It may make you afraid to do anything because you think everything you do is wrong. Do not deny that you may have guilt. Accept the fact that you were not a perfect child for your parents and that they were not perfect parents for you. Perfection is not a part of the human experience. Those who expect it of themselves and others only make the imperfections more difficult to live with. Above all, do not take time now to relive past problems.Look at your present situation as an opportunity to help your parents. Make the best of their present situation by helping them with the kind of care that they need—and that you (with others' help) can give.

Who Makes the Decision?
When your parents made the decisions for you during your childhood, they did not have to question their responsibility. They knew it was their job to feed, clothe, educate you— plus do all the other things necessary to get you launched into life. They may have had a little (or a lot) advice from their parents, other well-meaning adults, plus an occasional stepparent, but it was their responsibility to guide your life. They didn't need to read a book to tell them it was their job.

Life may not be so simple for you when the tables are turned. If you have brothers and sisters, you have a committee—and we all know how easily committees solve problems. However, if a family has already established a way of working together, it will have a pattern to follow as members face the critical decisions that must be made for aging parents.

> When Dad died, Mom seemed to know which of her five children to ask for help. One helped plan the funeral, another helped with insurance, some helped her with other business decisions. Patterns that we had established earlier helped when Dad died; they helped us kids reinforce our way of working together for decisions that would have to be made later.

1 • The Tables are Turned–on You

Sometimes having siblings can complicate decision making.

> Mom told me how she felt about some very important issues in what I regarded as a very serious conversation. We talked about what she wanted done if she became incapacitated or died. However, I later discovered that she had told my brother some very different opinions on the same subjects. Apparently she didn't intend to give either of us specific instructions; she was just talking abut her opinions at the moment. Needless to say, she caused some problems between my brother and me.

Even if you are an only child, others may consider themselves a part of the decision-making process for your aging parents. In some cases, no one wants to make the decision, though many may want to give advice. In other cases everyone may want to make the decision without advice or consent from anyone else. You already have a problem because your parents need help. Now you recognize that you may have a problem with the problem.

> When my father died I was the only one left to provide for my mother. She expected me to take care of her every need— just as Dad had done. That was problem enough! But only then did I realize how much I had depended upon talks with my father. I needed to have a visit with him as I worked through Mom's problem. My normal mourning process for my father complicated my ability to make decisions for my mother.
>
> I felt that I was responsible for the care of my parents, and I hoped that God would help me deal with the situation. God is still working on that.

In any self-help book on decision making you would be told to do things in proper order. But it is difficult to line up real life like chapters in a book. Things often seem to happen out of order. Sometimes you must make decisions now, and face the consequences later. That's okay. All decisions don't have to be permanent. By finding temporary solutions to the immediate problems, you can buy time to involve all of those who are a part of the decision making process and to find more options for long- term help. If you have the total responsibility for your parents, this book will guide you as you look at your specific situation. If this must be a group decision, it can help to set the agenda for those necessary meetings.

Be aware of some of the normal problems that must be a part of your present situation regarding your parents. Do not expect yourself to do everything exactly right—and do not expect perfection of others who are involved. Be comfortable with the idea that you have a problem, but remember that your parents are not the problem—the situation is.

Problems Big and Small

Often families will avoid the important issue by disagreeing on minor details. It is one way of avoiding the bigger, more painful facts. The human brain has a built-in overload clutch. When we have to face decisions that are too difficult, the clutch kicks in and shifts to minor issues that are easier to handle. At times we need that safety device to protect us from emotional stress. But we also need to know when it is time to confront the central issues.

I never realized how much I had depended on my parents for advice even as an adult, until I realized that they could not take care of themselves anymore—let alone take care of me. I had this strange feeling of wanting to ask them for advice on how to help my parents. It was hard to face the fact that they needed me now in the same way I had needed them for years.

1 • The Tables are Turned–on You

Look at your situation as if it were a TV show. Who are the main characters? the supporting cast? What is the conflict that gives the story a plot? Will the story have a happy ending or a tragic one? Or will it end with one of those conclusions that doesn't really resolve anything?

By seeing the events of your own life in this way, you can better understand the normal family conflicts you may face. You can see that someone has to take action to keep the plot moving.

> I had written the story of my mother's life. I did it just because it was something I wanted to do for my family and for my mother. The story was about her childhood, her parents and grandparents. When the time came for me to make decisions for my mother, I knew what she expected because it was all in her story. In one sense she told me what she needed me to do for her because I knew what she did for her parents.

There are some things that you need to be aware of.

First, you, and others who are involved in making these decisions, may have professional training and experience in handling such personal matters. Some of you may be very successful in the business world, but your professional abilities will not always be an asset in this family decision. In this case you are a son or daughter, a brother or sister. You are involved because of those family relationships, not because of the degrees on your office wall or your status among your peers. Don't expect other members of your family to let you take over because of your professional clout—and don't let others take over because they think they have an inside track on how to care for elderly people.

Having said that, do any members of your family have special training or contacts that can help you? If you have medical, legal, or other professionals in your family, their experience and contacts may be helpful to you. However, look at what they have as experience and information to help all of you reach a decision—not as authority to make the decision for you.

> I grew up as the baby sister in my family and am still seen as the kid by my brothers and sisters. The fact that I worked full time in a social-service agency for the elderly gave me no status in the family. The oldest brother was a pastor, another was an accountant. They held the power. They delayed getting the proper help for our parents for two years because they wouldn't consider the information I had to offer.

The situation regarding your parents will not be the only thing happening in your lives. Each one of you will still be a part of the normal activities that happen in everyone's life. You may have your own family, your spouse and your children, and any one (or all) of them may also need your full attention at this time. Your job will also be involved. You may have to deal with a move to a different city, a strike, longer working hours—all at the same time that you want to devote more attention to your parents. There is an old Chinese curse that says, "Give my enemy an interesting life." Your life may be too interesting right now.

> My husband and I had decided to adopt a child. As we got into the process we were told that it might be possible for us to adopt a family of three siblings. All of a sudden our lives were turned upside down. We had to face a total change in our financial situation. We had to think about a different house and a change in my work. Then my mother, who lived five states away had a stroke. She had to go to a nursing home—and I had to be the one who made the arrangements.

1 • The Tables are Turned–on You

Shortly after my mother-in-law died, my mother had a stroke and could no longer live alone. I never realized until then how much I depended upon talking to my wife about decisions. But my wife was dealing with her own mother's death, and it was hard for us to talk about my mother's situation. Yet my mother needed help then, and I had to give it.

My husband told me he wanted a divorce. The next day I got a phone call from my brother telling me that we had to make a decision about Mom going into a nursing home.

Seeing your parents become aged will be a reminder of your own future. You will remember your grandparents—and the conversations you heard between your parents as they had to deal with the situation that now faces you. You will wonder who will be responsible for you when you are the one who needs the protection of others. You will look at your own children—and probably be scared.

All of these things are a part of the normal life cycle. Take comfort in the knowledge that others just like you have weathered these storms and survived. There is hope.

Who Comes First?
First, let's consider the possibility that you are the sole, or the primary, decision-maker for your parents when they no longer take care of themselves. It is natural at such a time for your attention to be only on your mother and/or father. They are the ones who are in need. To think about yourself at a time when their requirements are much greater, seems selfish. However, to be the most effective in helping your parents, you need to think about yourself first.

An easy illustration: A hiker gets lost in the desert. Even though the hiker's life is in danger and every moment counts, you would not rush out looking for the one who is

25

lost until you prepare yourself to be of help. You need to take water, food, and medical supplies. You need backup support to assist you in a rescue. If you rush out into the desert without proper preparation, the rescue teams will need to look for two lost hikers instead of one.

So also in helping your parents in a difficult time of their lives. They need your help. They may be facing some of the most critical decisions in their lives, and they can't do it on their own. But if you rush in to help without preparing yourself, your help for your parents will be less effective. You may create so many problems in your own life that you will end up adding more burdens to the very people you want to help.

Caring as a Single Adult

If you are single, you may have a problem that no one will recognize except you; therefore you are going to have to be the one who explains your situation to others. Often other family members and friends assume that a single adult is the obvious one to take care of Mom and Dad because "she doesn't have anyone else to be responsible for," or "he's the only one who has the time."

> Because I had stayed single and stayed at home, the rest of the family assumed that I was totally responsible for our parents. They offered advice to me, and little else. When they came to visit Mom and Dad, I was the host and had to take care of them too. As far as they were concerned, they were on vacation.

In reality a single person has his or her time rationed and scheduled as much as those who have a spouse and children. You may have a "significant other." You may be healing from a broken marriage or a death and need special attention for yourself. You may have added commitments at work or in volunteer groups that you made because you had the time and energy to give—before you found out that your parents would need that time and energy. You may have physical and emotional limitations that others are not aware of.

The fact that you have other things to consume your time and use your energy does not mean that you cannot help your parents in their time of need. Often it is the busy people who are effective and capable of taking on more responsibility.

I have another word of preparation for a single person with no children. As you think about your parents and make decisions for them, you will be aware of the fact that you do not have children to do the same for you. This may cause you some concern. In this case, keep in mind that assisting your parents has a twofold advantage for you. First, you truly can help your parents. Second, you can become aware of the help you may need in your later years. Plan now. Talk to friends. Make a will, and name someone to have your power of attorney. Evaluate the insurance policies that include nursing-home care.

At the same time my father died I had a friend who also lost his father. Naturally we were a comfort to each other because we shared the same situation. Each of us was left with a widowed mother. But that's where the parallel ended. My parents had made plans for their own future. Mom knew what to do and how to do it because she and Dad had always shared their decisions. However, my friend's mother was helpless. She had never even thought about the fact that she might be left alone some day. She had never made financial plans. That experience taught me to prepare for my own future.

Caring as a Married Adult
Being married when you face the issue of making decisions

27

for your parents does not make the project any easier—just different. You must consult with and consider your spouse in each decision. At the same time, you'll find it helpful to have someone with whom you can discuss your personal feelings and obligations toward your parents.

However, it is possible that your spouse also has parents in the same situation, or who will be in that condition in a few years. As you and your spouse talk about your parents you will also have to consider your in-laws. Will you be able to provide money, time and energy equally for both sets of parents? Rarely will the situation be the same for both parents and in-laws. They may live in different areas. They will have unique needs and differing expectations. You may have learned to treat both sets of parents alike by sending the same gifts on special occasions and dividing your time between them on holidays. However, the separate-but-equal policy will probably not work when it comes to decisions about their needs when they are incapacitated.

You and your spouse may also have different views regarding your responsibilities. Before the two of you try to make decisions, talk about your experiences regarding the care of elderly people (for example, your grandparents and other older relatives). Understand how your feelings about those experiences will influence your decisions regarding your parents.

Also think about your relationship with your parents over the years. What happened during the years that you matured from an adult-to-child arrangement to that of adult-to-adult? Do you carry guilt or resentment? Have there been issues—such as money, manipulation, jealousy among siblings—that have left scars? Or have your parents given you special help and kindness that make you feel a deep sense of gratitude to them? Since they now are in need, are you grateful that you have an opportunity to help them? Your spouse needs to understand your feelings on these subjects in order to understand the decisions you make.

Consider the relationship between your spouse and your parents during the years of your marriage. Have there been misunderstandings or angry feelings that will make your spouse and your parents uncomfortable about the decisions being made? Does your spouse fear that your only goal is to bring your parents to live in your home?

> My mother and my wife never got along. There's no point in trying to find out which one was to blame—they just didn't like each other. But my mother lived over a thousand miles away; so we managed. Then my mother decided to move near us so I could take care of her. I admit she was a demanding person. The two years that she lived near us before her death were the most difficult years of my marriage.

Often people want to pretend they have a perfect family. Many have been taught that you don't hang out the family's dirty laundry for all to look at. But now you need to see your family relationships as they really are. If you are having difficulty doing this, talk to a counselor or pastor to get a realistic view of yourself and others in your family.

Do you and your spouse have a clearly defined and mutual understanding of your goals as a married couple for the next five years? Do you both have the same view of your financial situation, your job security? You will need to talk over these issues and others before you consider the major decisions regarding your parents.

Next think about your relationships with and responsibilities toward your own children and, perhaps, grandchildren. Problems never make appointments or present themselves at convenient times, and they often seem to come in clusters. About the same time that you must give your parents special attention that will demand more of your money, energy and time, your children may need help with tuition costs or support as they go through job changes or divorces. You will feel like the rope in a game of generational tug-of-war.

> My children thought my father was the perfect grandfather until he came to live with us. When he started asking them about the time they came home, and when he complained about their music and over-use of the telephone, he lost his hero status. And my kids lost someone that they could go visit to get a second opinion about life.

The choice is not between which of the generations you will help. You won't say, "I will forget my children and help my parents this year," or vice versa. Nor can you put your own life on hold as you expend your resources helping both parents and children. Your children may need to become a part of the team to provide support for their grandparents, and their needs also have to be considered.

All of these issues regarding yourself, your family and your job, may not have a direct influence on your decision about what to do for your parents when they can no longer live on their own. But these factors have an affect on you and therefore will be a part of your decision-making process. All of us need to take an emotional inventory every once in a while. Your need to reflect on yourself and to talk things over with your spouse and children will not only help you as you face your responsibilities for your parents. It will also be good for your relationship with your family and your understanding of yourself.

Evaluate Your Attitudes about Nursing Homes
Most of us approach the decision-making process with built-in attitudes that influence the results.

What is your attitude about nursing homes and other residences for the elderly? Do you see them as necessary evils or as away-from-the-rest-of-the-world places where old people can go to disappear? Are they a natural part of a community that includes schools, businesses, doctors' offices, churches, and the like?

Based on your own visits to such homes, stories you have heard from friends and families, movies you have seen and books you have read, do you like nursing homes? Or do you pray, "I hope I'll never live in a place like that"?

It is true that some facilities for elderly people are badly run. But it's also true that only the bad ones make the news. They are not representative of the total nursing home industry. Every type of business, every profession, has a long list of bad examples. Some doctors mistreat their patients. Some bankers steal from their customers. Some pastors are immoral with members of their congregation. Some restaurants serve food that makes you sick. But that shouldn't keep you from going to a doctor, keeping your money in a bank, joining a church, and eating in restaurants.

Do not let a few stories of mistreatment in nursing homes give you a negative view of all the facilities that care for elderly people. The great majority of homes for the elderly are operated by good people with high standards of care. Your job will be to find the best of the best.

Check Your Attitude about the Elderly

Next, what is your attitude about elderly people? Today *old* has become a bad word; the elderly are referred to as the "chronologically gifted." That seems to imply that there is something wrong with being old. I don't feel that way. Do you?

The Bible speaks of growing old as a blessing. In the book of Proverbs, the author wrote, "Long life is the reward of the righteous; gray hair is a glorious crown." Not all people would agree. The point is that age can be a blessing. That is the heart of this book: Can you help make your parents' old age good for them—and good for yourself?

Listen to yourself and others as you talk about nursing homes, wheel chairs, hearing aids, false teeth, walkers and medications. Some people speak of such things as bad—as signs of failure. In reality they are blessings for those who need them—and they are also blessings for those who love people who need them.

The purpose of this evaluation is not to determine how you should feel about old age, but how you *do* feel. If you try to force yourself to have a different attitude about the old—in case you think you need an attitude adjustment— you will put a stress on yourself that will make it difficult for you to care for your elderly parents. On the other hand, if you examine your attitudes and discover why you may have some negative opinions, you can change your attitude at its roots and grow in your ability to appreciate your parents in their elderly years.

Evaluate Your Attitude about Your Parents
Consider the specific attitudes that you have about your parents. Do not tell yourself—or let others tell you—what your attitudes should be. Start with an honest appraisal of your relationship with your parents and their relationship with you. If changes must be made, make them. But do not participate in a cover-up by pretending there are not, and never have been, conflicts in your relationship with your parents.

The beauty of family relationships is that people are closely involved in each others' lives. That means they share in the joys and the sorrows, the virtues and the vices. With friends, we can either select the people we will like or we can limit the friendship to areas that we agree upon. With family, what you see is what you get.

I never realized how peculiar my mother was until I had to help her find a place to live after Dad died. She didn't face reality and she never had—though I had never admitted it before. That was hard for me. But I had to go back in my memories to see how our family had covered her peculiarities before I could help her.

Rather than trying to be perfect in your relationship with your parents, try to avoid the extremes that can be disastrous for all concerned.

Watch for an overload of guilt. Often people will feel that they were unkind to parents in teenage or young adult years. Maybe they even had a time of separation from parents. Then when the parents become incapacitated, the children are filled with guilt. The parents may then recognize the guilt and use it to control the situation.

Parents also may feel guilty. They may have neglected or abused their children. They may carry guilt over a divorce or other family problem. Their guilt may make it difficult for them to accept honest attempts to help them. The guilt feelings of anyone involved in the situation will cloud the issue of providing the best possible care for your parents. If you sense that this could be a problem, try to resolve it with your parents. If not with them, seek help from clergy or a counselor so you can deal with your guilt and care for parents.

I lied to my mother. It bothers me that I did it, and it bothers me even more that I still defend it. See, she lived in Ohio, and my sister and I lived in Arizona. Mom needed to come live near us, but she didn't want to. So I told her that the doctor said she had to live in a hot, dry climate. That wasn't true. But it forced her to accept our decisions. It's worked out fine for her to live near us. But I am still bothered by the fact that I lied to her.

Watch for feelings of revenge. Many people carry anger for years and look for a chance to get even. We can see it in others, but rarely see it in ourselves. Listen to yourself talk. Do you excuse something you do or do not do for your parents by reminding yourself and others of how your parents failed you? Do you need to explain the bad things your parents did to you in order to defend your treatment of them now? Let's face it: you probably did not have perfect parents. They probably did not have perfect children. But old wounds need not be reopened now. If there have been difficulties in your relationship with your parents, be grateful that you now have an opportunity to develop a good family experience. Make the most of it.

Watch for overcompensation. Some people will react to previous problems by ignoring present opportunities to have a good relationship; others will overcompensate. Of course you need to help your parents. But you are helping them for the present and the future; you are not repaying them for the past.

I had a hard time dealing with an old father. I had always seen him as stronger than me both mentally and physically. And I had fought against his superior strength. I had said some pretty bad things to him.
Then when I saw him old and weak, I had no way to communicate with him. I couldn't argue anymore. I kept feeling that I needed to hug him and tell him I was sorry. It was rough. It still is, even though he died several years ago.

If you must make the decisions for your parents by yourself, give yourself some time for self-reflection first—even if it is only for a day. Find those strengths in yourself that will help you make good decisions. Find those weakness or problems in yourself that will make this job difficult for you. Then look for friends and confidants who can help you in the areas where you need help.

1 • The Tables are Turned–on You

Is This a Group Decision?

In many cases a group, rather than an individual, will have to make the decisions for incapacitated adults. In most cases that team will be brothers and sisters—the children of the person who must receive special care. In some cases there may be other members of the group: uncles and aunts, a spouse or long-term friend, and perhaps former in-laws who have kept a close relationship with the family. These people may not all have an equal vote; however, if they love the person whose life now needs direction, their concerns should be considered.

After Mom died, Dad found a special friend, Gladys. Most of the family accepted the friendship as a good thing— except for one brother who always worried that Dad would marry Gladys. He never did. When Dad had a stroke, Gladys had no legal responsibility to care for him. But I knew she wanted to still help him. And I knew that Dad still needed her friendship. We had to include her in the decisions. That added something else that we never expected: We became involved in taking care of Gladys as she aged.

In one sense a group decision may be easier to make. Instead of bearing the responsibility by yourself, you have others who can share the burden. Each additional person on the team adds more resources and experiences.

The time came when Mother had to leave the family home. We all knew it. The entire family was able to get together at one time, though we lived far from each other. We talked things over and decided that Mother should live near me. Everyone agreed. While we were together we also talked about the division of family treasures from our parents' home. We even made funeral arrangements. It was a natural thing for us to do.

Now I can take care of the day-to-day needs of my mother, knowing the entire family agrees about what is happening. I also know I won't be left alone to make decisions when she dies.

At the same time, groups have their share of drawbacks as well. One problem may be finding time for all who are involved to be together. In a day when many families are spread across a country, if not around the world, it is difficult enough to get a family quorum at weddings and funerals. Perhaps a conference phone call would help. Perhaps those who can meet together need to write down their concerns and make a list of possible solutions for your parents. Then those who live in other areas can be aware of the issues and help to make final decisions.

I was the only one in my family that left home, went to college, and moved around the country in my job. I maintained close contact with my parents by mail and phone and visited them regularly. They also enjoyed traveling to visit me. However, when they needed to sell the home where they had lived for fifty years and go to an assisted-living home, my brothers and sisters cut me out of the decision. They implied that I had left my parents and therefore no longer had a voice in providing for their care. I'm still hurt. I feel that my brothers and sisters were unfair to me.

Before your collective family can come to a conclusion, they must establish a way of working together. Consider the special needs of each person who is a part of the process. Do any have special financial, health or family problems? Will those personal concerns make it more difficult to participate in this family process? Are there old wounds in the family that

1 • The Tables are Turned–on You

could resurface during a time of tension? Will the need to make a decision for your parents provide a battleground for other family disputes? These kind of concerns (and the special situations in your family) must be considered and resolved—at least to the extent that they not cause more problems for your parents.

In some situations the term *dysfunctional family* seems to be redundant. If this is true in your case, it may be necessary to say, "Let's pretend that we all get along with each other so we can give our parents the best possible help." If you work together well as you share your concerns for your parents, you may solve some other problems while you are at it.

> Because everyone in my family had moved to different parts of the country we were seldom together. We had gotten into the habit of letting Mom act as our communication center. We would write to her instead of each other and she would pass the word around.
> When the time came to find another place for Mom to live, we had to be in direct contact with one another. It was a good experience for us. We became a family again. I remember the time my sister and I talked on the phone for almost an hour. As we hung up, she said, "I love you." We hadn't said that to each other for years.

When any group (especially members of a family) must make a decision, personalities always become a part of the decision. In this family crisis those personality issues may cause a problem because they may have a greater influence on the final action than the needs of the elderly people involved. Therefore, it is important that no member of the group start out by stating what she or he wants the final decision to be. Such a statement forces all the other members of the group to either agree or disagree with the aggressive one. Then the discussion is diverted from the facts that must be considered to the person who already has an answer. It is better for the group to consider all the possibilities, with none of the proposed solutions being identified with one person. Instead, concentrate on the needs of your parents. Some items on the list of possibilities will automatically be dropped. Others will be compared and refined. Finally a solution can be found by the group rather than by one who requires group approval.

> When we were children our family went through World War II together in Europe. We learned how to survive together. Since then we've had good lives, but that bonding experience from our childhood helped us as we worked together to care for our elderly parents. We knew we could do it because we knew we were a family.

Though I have compared your family meetings to that of a committee, don't let your discussion become like a meeting of the board of directors. Avoid taking votes. Discuss concerns and look for solutions that can be accepted by consensus rather than a majority. If the consensus cannot be reached on the first try, delay the decision as long as possible; your parents will need the support of all those who love them. Members of the family will also need to continue working together after the initial decision has been made. Let the fact that you need to work together in this decision establish a pattern that will help as you continue to care for your parents.

Finally, the group that makes the decision about where your parents will live will not disband once they come to a conclusion and the results are put into effect. Because your group will continue to work together as long as your parents are alive, it is worth taking the time to establish good decision-making habits. Identify and accept the natural leaders in the group. Accept the group's decision and avoid "I win—you lose" situations. Be open to making changes after the first solution has been tried: your parents' circumstances may change, the facility you chose may change, or you may have made a mistake the first time around. It happens all the time.

You Are Part of a Support System

Perhaps you are not responsible for making the decisions about caring for a person whom you love. For whatever reason, you may be on the second team in decision making. But even though you are not in the main loop, you can still be involved. You can still play an important part in the total care of the elderly person.

> Aunt Hattie really was not my aunt, but I called her that because she was important to me and I know I was important to her. I was the one who helped her many times when her own children were too busy to be bothered. But when the time came for her to go to a nursing home, they made the decisions. At first I was hurt. But I realized that Aunt Hattie had not made the choices that moved her far away from me. So I still kept in touch as best as I could. After all, she was still my aunt.

The best way of helping the elderly or handicapped person is to provide support for the person and the group who have the final authority. If you work against or around the decision makers, you may cause grief for the person you want to help. Accept the decisions of those in control and make the best of the situation. If you think others have made hurtful or unthinking decisions, be glad that you are there to ease the strain rather than add to it. Offer yourself not only to the patient but also to the others who are involved. Offer transportation, child care, and other support as needed.

Now You Are Ready
After you have given thought to your own situation in life, and after you have considered the situation of others who are involved in this decision, you are ready to turn your attention to your parents. As you collect the facts and the feelings about your parents and consider their needs, you may need to reevaluate many of the things mentioned in this chapter. Real life cannot be organized into sequential chapters like a book.

In all of this self-evaluation, be happy about two important things: First, you are there to help your parents. You may feel deep pain for them as you share their needs. But without you, their situation would be worse. You are an important part of their solution. Second, you are not alone. Be aware of how many other individuals and groups are available to give you primary and secondary help. Use their resources.

2

The Tables are Turned– on Your Parents

When the tables are turned on you, those same tables are also turned on your parents. They have to get used to the idea that you now have responsibility for them. They probably won't like having you run their lives. This is nothing against you personally, but from their side of the table you are their *child*—even if you are sixty years old. You will need patience as you help them understand that they are not being punished because of their limited abilities. They are not failures because they are dependent upon you.

In the previous chapter you were asked to think about yourself before you made decisions for your parents. In this chapter you will be asked to think about your parents before you make decisions for them. You first had to understand your own involvement in the total picture so you could explain yourself to your parents and others. Now you also

need to understand your parents' view of life, so your decision considers their needs as well as your own. The greatest
temptation for those who make decisions for others is to consider their own needs before the needs of those under their
responsibility. Remember two simple facts: What is best for
your parents will eventually be the best for you. And, what is
best for you might not be best for your parents.

Often we look at our parents and wonder if we will
become like them. Will we gain the weight (then perhaps
lose it), lose the hair (then perhaps replace it), turn gray
(then perhaps restore the original color), develop the characteristics of our parents? If I knew the answers to those
questions, I'd be writing a different book. However, the
ideas and exercises suggested in this chapter may be helpful for you not only as you make decisions regarding the
care of your parents, but also as an evaluation of yourself
as you move through a new stage of life. This phase will be
one more learning experience for you, with your parents as
the teacher and you as the student. Even though you may
be in charge of present events, as you help your parents
you will be aware of the time when you will need to let
others help you. Give help to your parents in the way you
would want to be helped—that's the Golden Rule updated
to be the Golden-Ager Rule.

Helping my parents as they grew older was easy for me.
It all seemed natural. Then I realized something: I knew
how to care for my parents because I was there to watch
them do the same for their parents. But my children are
spread across the country. They will not learn what I
learned unless I make an effort to share with them the
responsibility I have now for their grandparents. That's
not going to be easy, but I know it is necessary for my
sake—and for my children's sake too.

2 • The Tables are Turned–on Your Parents

The Rise and Fall of Independence

To many, losing independence is a sign of failure, punishment or rejection. Often we view the experiences of youth as positive, while those of the aged are seen as negative—even though both are natural. Shakespeare recorded the rise and fall of independence in *As You Like It.* He saw life as starting with "mewling," "puking" and "whining." Then life becomes great as one becomes a lover, soldier, and judge. But it ends "sans teeth, sans eyes, sans taste, sans everything."

The negative view of the loss of control in old age may cause two problems for you as you try to help your parents. First, your parents may see themselves as failures. They didn't plan to become dependent again; they feel responsible for their condition and they regret having to rely on others. You need to understand that they will need help in accepting their situation.

But the bigger problem may be your own view of aging. Some people say very bluntly, "I don't like old people." To many, old people are not interesting, not pleasant to look at or touch, and sometimes they don't even smell good. You will be in conflict with yourself if you feel a sense of responsibility to help your parents and at the same time resent their physical and mental inadequacies. This tension in you will make you less effective in helping your parents and cause anger that will spill over into other areas of your life. Therefore you need to understand for yourself (and in cases where it is possible help your parents understand) the rise and fall of independence.

Though this book is aimed at the major decision about arranging a place for your parents to live when they can no longer take care of themselves, that facet of their lives is only a part of the major changes they'll experience as they go from independence to dependence.

In order to understand the rise of independence, study the

list below. It contains the signs of change from dependence to independence as a newborn baby grows to become a toddler, a child, a youth and finally an adult.

Ability to protest
Ability to feed yourself
Ability to walk
Verbal communication
Ability to say no
Bladder and bowel control
Ability to dress yourself
Make decisions about use of time
Make decisions about use of money
Place your own order at a restaurant
Get a key to the house
Choose your own friends
Decide for yourselves about going to church
Get your driver's license
Live on your own
Provide for your own financial support
Choose your own doctor, dentist, etc.
The ability to provide for others

Most of the maturation experiences on the above list happen gradually. Some of them include a "big day," but most often we eagerly anticipate these steps of independence only to discover that they have passed with hardly a notice.

My oldest son came home from a school event one night when he was sixteen to find me still sitting up reading (so it would appear that I was not waiting for him). As we talked, he said, "Dad, I hope you won't feel bad if I tell you something." Statements like that terrify parents of teenagers, but I assured him I was ready for anything. "As I walked from the bus stop," he said, "I thought about what would happen if all of you were gone when I came home. I mean you and

2 • The Tables are Turned–on Your Parents

Mom and the house and everything—and I was on my own. And I decided I had reached the point where I could probably make it by myself."

Though in fact that son was still partially dependent on his mother and me for many years, he knew he had reached an important step. He could have made it on his own if he had to. It was a good moment for him—and for me. The point is that sometime in the future that same son and I may have to have a similar but opposite conversation. I may have to say, "I can no longer make it by myself." Growing up and gaining independence is as natural as growing old and losing independence.

> I realized that I was an adult the first time I bought toilet paper. Before that it had always come with the room— the place provided by parents and school. Now I realize that when I stop buying toilet paper I will know that I am becoming dependent again. It will again come with a room provided by someone else.

Consider the above list again. Each event that was a sign of independence can be reversed to become a sign of dependence. If both you and your parents can accept the signs of loss of dependence as being as natural and necessary as the process of becoming dependent was, you will be able to be much more help to them—and they will be in a good situation to accept and appreciate you help. The reverse list is not as orderly as "The Rise of Independence." Not all people share all of the experiences, but there are generalities that most people who live to an old age will experience.

Cannot help take care of others
Loss of sight and/or hearing
Loss of bowel and/or bladder control
Can no longer drive a car

Aging Parents

Can no longer live alone
Can no longer chose friends, doctor, church, etc.
Cannot dress yourself
Cannot feed yourself
Cannot remember recent events
Cannot walk
Needs financial assistance
Cannot make decisions
Cannot get out of bed
Not aware of what is happening
Does not recognize loved ones
Cannot breathe without help
Needs total life-support systems

The one-day-old baby and the incapacitated elderly person have a lot in common: both are human beings who need respect and love, and (for those of us who believe in eternal life) both have a future.

Enjoying your aged parents is not always easy. It helps if you can understand that their infirmities are natural and not blame them for what they cannot control.

I remember that I used to get angry at my mother because her hands trembled. I would tell her to stop shaking her hands. She tried. She would hold on to the arms of her chair or try to keep her hands folded. But it didn't work. I told her terrible things: that I wouldn't invite her friends over unless she promised to keep her hands still, or that she couldn't have coffee if she shook the cup and spilled it. Now my hands shake because I have the same disease my mother had. How I wish I could ask her to forgive me!

Independence is an important phase of life, but it is something we pass through—like puberty. Likewise, other parts of life that we often seen as goals—such as health, success, power, wealth— are more accurately seen as phases that come and go. The value we gain from life comes from living through the phases—not in holding onto them.

Understand that your parents have already developed their attitudes about age. What they think about it is what you have to deal with.

Across the Generation Gap

A generation gap is a sign of progress. You are different from your parents because you grew up in a different era and in different circumstances than they did. The same may be said of our children. The world changes and each generation must change with it.

One simple sign of the generation gap is in your understanding of our changing language. To your parents, a CD is probably a certificate of deposit. To you and your children it is probably a compact disc. You can probably still enjoy singing, "Don we now our gay apparel," but don't be surprised if your children snicker.

But a lot more than language has changed in the world since your parents developed their values, their expectations of life, and other mindsets that influence the way they make decisions. And while they may have kept up with the times in many ways, their points of reference still come from childhood. Some who now travel by jet remember the first time they saw an automobile. Some who now live in high-rise condos remember a farmhouse with no plumbing.

The more adjustments people have made in some areas of their lives, the more stability they need in others. One of my favorite parish stories is about an older couple who complained about a new hymnal being used by our congregation in the early 1970s. He, a retired corporation executive, was wearing beads. She was wearing a polyester pantsuit. But they still wanted to use the old hymnal that they had used for the last fifty years. Their uniform was modern; their hearts were traditional.

Aging Parents

I was always frustrated when I made my duty visit to Uncle Alfred and Aunt Helen. They lived in the past—no TV, no newspaper, radio for weather reports only. We couldn't talk about anything because we lived in different worlds. Then I learned how to communicate with them.

Their house was set far back from the street. When I got out of my car I would recite the current year. Then, with each step I would subtract five years. By the time I reached their door, I was at 1920—right where they lived. After that, I began to enjoy my visits with them. I learned a lot about what life was like long before I was born. Finally, I learned about the tragic event that caused them to put a lock on time.

If I did anything to help them, it was because I walked back to their world and did not demand that they catch up with mine.

Look at the differences between the way you look at life and the way your parents see things—and respect those differences. If possible, make the decisions by your parents' standards. If not, try to explain why a new set of rules are in operation. If your parents cannot understand, you can at least understand why they have a different point of view and do your best to make your decisions fit into their world.

For starters, consider the value of money from the time your parents first earned a dollar until now. People who worked for a dollar a day (or saw their parent do it) will have a different attitude about life than those who started out paying five dollars for a hamburger, fries, and a soft drink. Although they may have learned to leave a twenty percent tip after a meal, that does not mean it makes sense to them. Talking about money with your parents will be difficult if you are referring to a 1995 dollar and they are thinking about a 1935 dollar.

Next, realize that you may have an inaccurate view of

your parents' wealth—or lack thereof. Depending on their attitudes, they may think they are rich if they have $5,000 in investments. Or they may consider themselves poor if they have $500,000. Don't let their lifestyle fool you. Some people are rich because they act as if they are poor; others are poor because they act as if they are rich.

> When I was growing up, my parents never talked about money in front of the children. As far as I know they never even talked to each other about it. That caused the major problem for me when I had to help Mom move to a nursing home. I had to find out how much money she had and what her monthly income was. But by that time I had no way of finding out what her priorities were and what choices she would have made with the money that was available.

Remember how your parents talked about money in your presence when you were a child at home. Some families discuss every detail, every dime of the family's business with their children. Some do not even discuss it between husband and wife. You may be exactly like your parents because you were influenced by them. Or you may have changed because you are now also influenced by your spouse and the way their family dealt with money issues. Your education and work experience may also have given you a different attitude about money.

Even though your parents may no longer be able to handle money, most will still be aware of it. Some may feel relieved to hand over the care of the checkbook to someone else. Others will see it as another sign of their lost independence. Most of us, though, feel better if we have some pocket money; don't put your parents in the position of having to ask you for money—whether it is yours or their own. It is also best to avoid the symbolism of a weekly or monthly allowance. Find a way to transfer funds so that it is clear you are acting merely as custodian of their money.

There is another important change of attitudes across the generation gap. As you collect information about places where your parents might live, you will be swamped with brochures from happy-sounding places likes Rolling Hills Retirement Center, The Forum, and many other places with words such as *manor, village, villa, hills* and other just-this-side-of-heaven sounding names. But your parents will not be fooled by the cleverness of the public-relations squad. They know you are talking about nursing homes.

Understand that each of us keeps our own mental dictionary. As we live longer and have more experiences, we add to the definitions by listing new meanings. But we always keep the first definition—based on our first impression—and react from it as we deal with a changing world. As people grow older, and it becomes harder to keep up with recent events, they return to the first definition recorded in their memory. One of the clearest examples of this is seen in our attitude toward institutions for elderly people.

If your parents have memories from the thirties and forties in rural America, they may even think in terms of the county poor farm. Even those who have never seen a poor farm may have heard about it from parents or grandparents. It was the sign of ultimate failure, the threat used to motivate lazy teenagers and middle-aged daydreamers. It was the reason not to take a vacation or buy a new car. "You'll end up in the poor house!" was a more motivating threat than hell itself; all your neighbors would know you lived at the poor farm, while hell still offered a degree of confidentiality. (If you'd like a more intense lesson on the reality of the poor farm, I'd recommend reading *The Poorfarm Fair* by John Updike.)

The fear of the poor farm was not just the personal poverty but the belief that your family had abandoned you. One of the fears of those who didn't have children was that they would be residents of the poor farm—even if they had money—because there simply was no other place to go. Others were afraid they would be abandoned by their children and have no other choice.

Older people can have real fears about the changes that will occur in their lives when they can no longer live on their own. Those fears can be relieved by honest information. But anxieties are not based on reality and therefore cannot be relieved by reality. If you sense a deep anxiety in your parents about places where elderly people now live, deal with it from the roots in their lives that gave them the first definition of homes for the elderly. You can't yank an anxiety away from a person; in fact, pressure only makes them hold onto it more tightly. But they can be given new assurances that help them relax and release the old anxieties.

Also understand that nursing homes themselves have changed dramatically since the time your parents first visited one. I was first exposed to places for elderly people in the late fifties. Most of them were old houses, unmodified for their new use and unregulated by local governments. Too many people were crammed in rooms far too small. Doors were too narrow for wheelchairs and the bathrooms too few and ill equipped for people with physical limitations. If your parents visited homes such as these they may have made a strong promise to themselves that they would never go to a nursing home. They may have even made you as a child or young adult promise that you would never put them in one. You won't remember that promise because it probably seemed silly at the time—but they were serious and they will remember.

Grandma always said she would never live in a nursing home. I remember her saying so at family gatherings even when it didn't fit into the conversation. She seemed to be giving notice to everyone that she had made up her mind and the issue was settled. However, when no one in the family could provide the around-the-clock care she needed, she had to go to a nursing home. I dreaded visiting her because I thought she would be angry or depressed because her greatest fear had become a reality. But I was pleased to find that she was content with her new surroundings She handled it well by telling me, and others, that she was not in a nursing home. It may have been nothing more than old-fashioned denial. Or it could be that the place where she was staying, which was very nice, really was not a nursing home according to Grandma's definition.

A third area in the generation gap that may cause difficulty is family expectations. Your parents may still be operating on, or may revert back to, a farm or small-town mentality that believes each family must take care of its own. They may not be aware that most people no longer have large homes with extra bedrooms. They may not realize that your job, or your spouse's, might require you to move at any time.

All of our family roots were from northern Europe, but my daughter-in-law was Hispanic. When I mentioned to her where I would move in the event of my husband's death, she was upset. She said that I would live with her and our son. And even though my son said he would help me find a place, she protested that families had to stay together. I would have to live with them.

Recall family stories about your grand- and great-grandparents. Did they live in the homes of their children? Are there good and/or bad memories in the family from the experiences?

2 • The Tables are Turned–on Your Parents

Family responsibilities have also been affected by two generations of frequent divorce and remarriage in our society. Each family must look at special situations that must be considered as parents grow older.

My parents were divorced forty-five years ago and never saw each other much after that. Dad had remarried and moved away. Mom came to live with us fifteen years ago. Then Dad's second wife died and he was left alone. When I went to see him, I realized he would have to come to live with me. But that meant Mom and Dad would have to share a room. There was no other solution in my home; I was already taking on extra expenses, so I couldn't buy another house. At first I thought about the morality of it, but that became a minor problem as I dealt with the practicality of the situation.

Recognize that your parents may have many other views from their generation that do not match with your own. They may think that doctors should still make house calls. Being forty miles away from where you live may seem like a long distance to them, and living six states away might seem to make visits impossible. Identifying all the issues that cause a generation gap between you and your parents does not mean that you must move across the gap to decide things according to their system. Quite the contrary! But you can recognize the problem and understand their frustration as they deal with a world that no longer seems like home.

Retiring from Retirement
A basic rule of life: It's easier to upgrade than it is to downgrade. It's easier to change from poverty to wealth than from wealth to poverty. It's easier to make a transition from sickness to health than from health to sickness.

It's also much easier to make the change from dependence to independence than from independence to dependence. As children become adults, they test their ability to go on their own. If they fall flat on their face this week, they at least learned something in the process and they can try again next week. They can accept a temporary setback because they see a future ahead of them.

The process reverses itself at the other end of life, when older people reflect on the times when they managed their own lives and feel apprehensive about a time when they will relinquish that control. The most critical question for people as they grow older—and for their loved ones who must help them—is, When do I quit trying and allow others to help me? If we give up too soon we hasten our own helplessness. If we resist help from others or from medical devices—even such aids as canes and walkers—we cause ourselves unnecessary pain and limit our own abilities. It is difficult enough for us to make such a decision for ourselves. It is even more difficult if we must make the decision for someone else.

My mother was always very active. In fact, I remember that I would often tell her to do less—not to clean the top cabinets, not to wash windows, and things like that. But after she had a series of mini-strokes, she stopped doing anything. She would just sit in her chair all day. I'd ask her to get the mail, or I'd stay late at the office just to see if she would get up to fix her own dinner. She would get angry and tell me that I wasn't taking good care of her.
She was also upset at her doctor. He had told her that she should mow the lawn because the lawn mower would be like a walker for her and would help her become more mobile. The doctor and I both felt a need to keep her walking. But I wondered if we were asking her to do the impossible.

2 • The Tables are Turned–on Your Parents

As difficult as it is to help aged people to accept a gradual loss of physical abilities, that problem is easy when compared to the gradual loss of decision-making abilities. A person rarely goes from full mental ability to total loss of self-determination overnight. The change is not only gradual; it is also inconsistent and selective. One day a person may be lucid and capable of responsible decisions. On another day the same person may be unable to follow even a simple conversation. A person may speak intelligently on one subject and be off-the-wall on others.

I visited Aunt Agnes because I knew she loved company and liked to talk. She seldom knew who I was. She told me wild stories about deciding whether or not to get remarried and have more children. I just listened and let her talk. One day the subject of investments came up. I was so tuned out of the conversation that I don't know if she mentioned it or I did. But suddenly I knew Aunt Agnes was lucid. She explained the relationship of the bond and stock markets. Though I thought I was above average in my knowledge of investments, I found myself listening to her opinions. She told how she and her first husband had made investments together, and she made suggestions about current investments based on information she had heard on a TV program. I went home that day with a new understanding of what happens in the human mind—and I knew we'd have something to talk about during our next visit.

I looked forward to visiting Edna in the nursing home. She was 101, had been bedridden for eleven years, and was in constant physical pain. But her mind was sharp. On one visit as I entered her room she recognized me and said, "It's good to see you. I was just thinking, Does anyone know the origin of God? What do you think about it?"

Aging Parents

Even though you may need to make the decision for your parents, you will no doubt want your parents' advice or consent, and you will hope for cooperation. For the moment it might seem that your job would be easier if your parents would just accept your decision without question. In the long run, however, you will be grateful that your parents still have the mental capacity to object to what you want to do.

You, and those who will help you, must evaluate how much your parents can understand and participate in deciding what must be done. You need to draw on whatever ability they have; yet you cannot operate under a cloud of guilt when the decision does not agree with their wishes.

One way to help your parents use the abilities they still have is to work with models that they understand. Most people have spent a long time planning for their retirement. They have made financial arrangements and have considered health, family, and personal preferences. They have probably discussed their plans with investment advisers, those who know the facts about Social Security and retirement funds, and perhaps doctors and lawyers. They may also have discussed their plans with other family members, friends, and counselors. Use their experiences (and your own) to help them understand what is happening to them now: they are retiring from retirement.

Just as it was necessary to give up the job in order to retire, it is necessary to give up certain things when one retires from retirement. Priorities for the second retirement are different than the first. Money and activities were important as they planned to retire. Attitudes, especially the ability to accept help from others, are more important as they plan to move from retirement into a new phase of life. Some will see the need for help and ask for it. Some will deny that need and refuse help.

Mom hid from all of us the fact that Dad had Alzheimer's.

We noticed that she always drove the car, but we also knew Dad couldn't see too well anymore. Then I noticed that she would answer questions addressed to Dad. My only reaction was a promise to myself that I would not do the same to my husband. When we finally realized that Dad was not operating on all cylinders anymore, Mom denied it. We could have helped him much sooner and more easily, if we did not have to work around Mom.

Realize that many elderly people refuse help because they do not know what resources are available to them. They continue to operate on past needs and past abilities. To help them accept a change, you need to let them know that they have other options.

The "More-So" Syndrome

As people grow older, their personal characteristics often become exaggerated. If they were kind and patient during their middle- age years, they become more kind and patient as they grow old. If they were intolerant and subject to bursts of anger in their younger years, it will get worse as they grow older. This is called the "more-so" syndrome. What they did before becomes more- so as they grow older.

My mother always had a positive attitude in life. Even though she had many problems—my brother died when he was 14, and she had some health problems all of her life—she did not feel sorry for herself. That attitude was the greatest blessing of her old age. I loved to go see her in the nursing home. She always had something good to say about the staff or the food. I would hear the other residents complaining, and I'd thank God for my mother's good nature.

My dad never did enjoy life. When things were going bad,

he blamed everyone else. When things were going well, he would try to guess what the next problem would be. When he got old I had a hard time being with him. As I drove to see him, I learned to make a game of it by guessing what he could gripe about today.

The "more-so" syndrome has its exceptions. Some people do mellow out as they grow older. Circumstances will cause some people to change bad habits. Others will lose some of the beauty they had— often because of health setbacks.

Evelyn had always been the model of what a little old lady should be. She was neat and clean. She was mentally alert. Most of all she was kind and gentle—everyone's image of the perfect grandmother. Then she had a stroke. She became angry and abusive. She embarrassed her family and friends by her language when they took her out. It hurt all who loved her to see what had happened to her.

The message for you as you accept responsibility for your parents is to accept them as they are. They may be able to make some improvements, or they may lose some of the virtues they have. Regardless, they need you—and you need them.

Seeing my parents grow old and become childish again helped me understand them and myself. They became dependent again at the time of life when I thought I had everything working the way I wanted. I was tempted to think that I had learned to handle everything. But again my parents became my teachers. I could not control my future any more than I had controlled my past. I learned to live for the day and make the most of it and help my parents enjoy each day that they could.

—— 3 ——

Your Answer Needs
a Zip Code

The place where your parents will live will need to provide health care, therapy, accessibility to family and friends, and other options needed by many elderly people. In the natural rush to find help for your parents, the temptation is to head for the Yellow Pages and collect information on all the agencies and institutions that provide care for the elderly. That must be done—but not yet.

Before you can decide where your parents will live in terms of the type of housing they need, you must decide what state and what city would be the best suited for them. The place where they will live needs a Zip Code.

Stay Where They Are

A basic concept of decision making is: If it's not broken, don't fix it. If your parents have lived in the same area for some time, and have enjoyed being there, why move them? While it may be necessary for them to change addresses, they could be able to keep the same Zip Code.

Weigh the importance for your parents of staying in their present locality. How many of the following reasons apply to your situation and how important are they in making a decision? What other reasons for staying should be added for your specific situation?

Being near other family members

Perhaps few—or none—of your parents' immediate family live in the area. However, your parents may have many cousins, nephews, and nieces in the vicinity. Will it be helpful to your parents to be near their extended family? Is the number of relatives large enough to remain helpful even if some die or move away?

Being near family can mean different things for different people. Family in its most ideal configuration offers love, encouragement, and care. Remaining near family can give a person a feeling of security and interdependence.

Of course, not all families fit the happy definition of people who love and care for each other. Know your family history. Is their a long-standing feud that has never been resolved, a divorce or a marriage that split the family, a family business that went bankrupt? Such resentments and bad memories might make it a good idea for your elderly parents to move to a new area and be free from the daily reminders of old problems.

Being near friends

Do your parents have long-term friendships that are more important to them than some family relationships? Is the network of friends large enough to still be helpful if some died, became ill, or moved away?

If your parents want to stay in their present neighborhood because of their many friends there, it might be good to see what plans the friends have. After all, they are growing older too.

Keeping the same doctor and other medical personnel
Have your parents had a long-term relationship with their doctor, dentist, etc.? Will those people probably remain in practice in their community?

> Mother had to move to a different state because of her health. The one thing that helped her accept the move was that she liked her new doctor. Since her health was the reason she had to move, the new doctor was the key to her feeling good about the move.

Might it be necessary for your parents to move to another area where more specialized medical care may be available? Is their present care a plus or a minus to their total health picture?

Maintaining special attachments to their present community
Do your parents have the "old home place," a local cemetery where a child is buried, or other important sentimental attachments that could not be replaced in other areas? Are these things important for them on a regular basis? Could their need for them be replaced by pictures and other memorabilia that would help them identify with earlier parts of their lives?

> When I talked to Dad about selling the farm and taking life easy, he told me that if he sold the place he would have to clean out all the farm buildings that were filled with four generations of stuff. "It would be easier just to stay here and die and let someone else take care of all of that," he said. That's exactly what he did. And as we sorted through

all the family collectibles we realized that he had been right. It had been easier for him to stay where he was.

I was surprised when my mother said she wanted to move to another state. She had spent her entire life within a few miles of the house where she was born. But she recognized that she needed a change. In her old neighborhood she had nothing to do but get older. In a new neighborhood she would need to make new friends and try new things. It was a good decision for her.

Remaining in the same church

Has church or synagogue involvement been an important part of your parents' lives? Do they feel needed in their congregation? Is their relationship to the church dependent upon one person—such as a pastor who might leave—or upon a larger group of people who could offer support?

Is their congregation changing as it tries to speak to a new generation? Sometimes it is difficult for the old time members of a church to accept change in a place where they have lived a long time. Yet those same people could accept and enjoy the different activities of another congregation in another area because they are not a part of the new church's history.

Weighing the Choices

Often a single reason for remaining in a certain area seems so important that the idea of moving is automatically rejected. However, good decision making must be based upon considering all the facts and giving a value to each one. As strong as the desire might be to stay in their present community, other needs may have to out-rank it.

Your parents' home may not be near hospitals or emergency service. To remain there might solve one need, but create others.

3 • Your Answer Needs a Zip Code

I always worried because my parents still lived on the farm, twenty miles from a hospital. However, when Dad had what turned out to be a minor problem they had to call 911. It was a relief to know that the ambulance with trained emergency technicians could be at their home on the farm and could get him to the hospital in no more time than it would have taken to get through city streets.

Some people must move to be in a dryer or a warmer climate. Others need to move away from an area that has special pollution problems because of factories or heavy traffic. Some have allegeries built up over long years of living in one place. The only choice is to move.

The doctor didn't mince any words. He told us that if Mom remained in the cold, wet climate where she had lived all of her life, she would die within a year. In a warm dry place she could live well for many years.

Even though your parents may have friends and relatives in their present neighborhood, none of them may feel the responsibility, or have the ability, to provide the daily contact and support that your parents need. While an elderly person will rank closeness to extended family and to friends as important, those relationships do not always provide the basic needs.

If your parents now live in a rural area or small town, they probably have a lot of support in the community. People know each other. Someone will phone or drop by every day. These things are important for elderly people. However, smaller communities cannot offer the professional resources of organizations and activities for elderly people. They cannot support groups for the aged who have special physical or emotional needs. They will not have as many agencies to provide home health care or respite, hospice, and other important services. There is a trade off between the advantages of small town versus the big city. Neither offers everything. Both offer something. The individual needs and values of your family will have to be considered as you make the choice.

Can You Go Home Again?

Often retirement, or retirement from retirement, gives people an opportunity to go home again. Many older people have moved many times and many miles from the place of their birth. As they grow older the memories of their childhood become more clear in their minds. They become more aware of their roots and they may realize how much they are like their parents. All of this may make them feel a need to go back to the place where they were born.

But can you really ever go home again? It all depends.

My wife's parents made it easy for us. They had spent most of their adult lives in the Twin Cities. When they retired, they moved back to the small town where my mother-in-law had lived as a child. They both loved it. Mom renewed old friendships and treated distant cousins like brothers and sister. Dad felt at home. Now that they will have to move to a nursing home our job is much easier. They already know most of the people in the home. And everyone else in town comes to visit them. When my parents retired and went to Arizona, they loved it—for about twenty-five years. But they both lived longer than they expected. When they had to give up their home, they decided to go back to St. Louis. They wanted to return to the life they had lived before they retired. But they couldn't move back to the old neighborhood because it had changed; it was no longer a safe place for them to live. Dad went back to the place where he had worked—and no one knew him. They were guests in the church where they once had been family. After ten months they moved to a retirement home back in Arizona.

Each family has its own story. Some return home and find that the old neighborhood has changed; so it is not home any more. Others go back and find that their home town hasn't changed a bit—but they have. They don't fit in anymore. Still others go back to the place of their childhood and find that it has kept up with the times. They like the new life in the old town.

In a time when one of every five families moves every year, few families have a place to call home. Even our immediate families become extended families in a geographical sense. Often if the oldest generation either remains in that place that everyone thinks of as home, or returns to that place, it is easier for all of the second and third generations to come back to see them. The second generation will come back to visit their parents and at the same time attend school and family reunions, renew old friendships, and bring the third and fourth generations to examine the family roots.

The five adult children in my own family ended up calling five different states home. We are probably typical. It is easier for the siblings and their children in such a family to see each other if they have a place back home where they can meet. The older generation can benefit from that need for a place called home.

Off to a New Start
If you think that all old people want to remain at, or go back to, the place of their childhood, forget it. Look at the large retirement settlements in Florida, Arizona, Arkansas and other areas with moderate climates. What you may think of as the older generation probably does not match the reality. They are different from their parents. Many of today's people in their senior years move to new places and do new

things. The bumper sticker that says, "I am spending my children's inheritance," is a statement of fact for many older people.

Granted, most of the on-the-move older people are those in their first retirement. They have the health, the money, and the interest to do new things. Moving to a new area, meeting new people, and doing new things gives them a new lease on life.

Does this same principle apply to the second retirement, when older people are more limited by physical and mental abilities? In some cases it can. You will need to know your parents and how they will react. Sometimes they will surprise you.

Dad had become very demanding in his older years. He terrorized Mom and her sister, Aunt Lilly, who lived with them. He made them wait on him. He didn't want anyone else in the house other than the three of them. It was bad. Then the two sisters died within a few weeks of each others. We panicked at the thought of putting Dad in a nursing home, but we had no choice. When he found out that his nasty ways wouldn't work there; he changed tactics. He became Mr. Nice Guy! He talked to people. He learned to say things like "Please" and "Thank you." He was a pussy cat. He actually liked the social events in the nursing home. I didn't know an old person could adjust that well.

For some old people a move to a new situation is a good thing. It gets them out of a rut. It helps them live in the present and look to the future, rather than rerun all the events of the past. For others a move to a new area makes no difference.

My mother had become a social recluse. She wouldn't or

couldn't talk to anyone. She lived in her own little world. Often she ignored me. I finally had no choice but to move her to a home near me—two thousand miles from where she had lived. It didn't make any difference to her, and it was a lot easier for me. She doesn't miss anything from her previous home, because she has forgotten all of it.

Look at the Finances

You've already considered the cost of family members traveling to visit your parents. That is an important part in your selection of a place for your parents to live. There are two other financial matters that are affected by their Zip Code.

Different states have different health-care programs. Some offer better coverage than others. Some have different requirements. If the possible places that you might choose for your parents are in different states, be sure to check the health and elder care provided by each.

Next, states have different income tax rates—some even have none. If your parents still have an income large enough to give you a concern about the amount of tax they will pay, consult the tax figures for each of the states that you are considering as a possible place of residence for your parents.

Pick a Place

Having too many options may be frustrating. If there is no obvious place where your parents should live, don't put a map on the wall and throw a dart to select the area for them. Make the best of the options you have. Get out a map and trace the normal business and vacation routes that those who will visit your parents will normally follow. You may find there is a place where the lines cross—a place where more members of your family would be able to visit your parents. That sounds like a good spot.

The next best choice would be the place where your

parents—and the rest of you—would like to vacation. If they live near a good vacation spot, members of the family can combine vacation with family visits.

4

Which Floor?

Imagine that making a decision regarding a place for your parents is like a shopping trip. The point of shopping is to match, as closely as possible, what you need with what is available and affordable. As you look for the best living arrangements for your parents you should know what they need now and have a good idea about their future needs. You may not be able to find exactly what you need, where you need it. That's where shopping comes in: you'll want to look for the best you can get for the price you can pay. By taking the time to shop, you may also find that you have more and better options than you had counted on.

Pretend that you are standing in the lobby of a four-story building that has brought together all of the possible places that you might pick for your parents. Each floor of the building has a different level of care. Your first step is to decide which level of care your parents need. With that established, you can visit that floor to inspect the many different institutions that offer the kind of care that meets their needs.

In this chapter, we will stay at the information desk in the lobby. In the following four chapters we will explore the first floor, then get on the elevator and see what other options are available for your parents.

First Floor: Home Care

All of those who work with elderly people agree that it is best to keep them in private homes as long as possible. Most people are more content in homes, and in many cases it is less expensive to help families keep their elderly parents in their own home than it is to put them in places supported by tax and/or insurance money.

Is it possible for your parents to remain in their own home? move to your home? or live in the home of another relative or friend? The answer to those questions may be a very loud no or an equally loud yes. But before considering the specifics (that's for the next chapter), take some time to evaluate the possibilities.

First, the loud no. There may be obvious reasons why some elderly people cannot remain in a private home. They may require medical attention that friends and family cannot provide at home. Their emotional or mental state may make it impossible for them to be with family. Situations about a house, or about the people presently living in a house, may automatically make it impossible for elderly people to remain in, or to move into, the home.

However, in some cases the no may be less emphatic. There may be problems in having your parents remain in a private home, but there will be some problem with every possible solution. The problems of being in a private home may be fewer than the problems of other possible solutions; of all the choices it might be the best option available. You may want to browse around this level of care to see what help is available for those who keep elderly people in their own homes.

> After she fell we all assumed that mother would have to be in a nursing home. But it seemed everything went wrong: she wasn't happy, she had a difficult roommate. I could not take the stress of a job and help her also. She demanded more and more, and we all understood how she felt. We tallied up the cost of the nursing home and it was more than my take-home pay. My brothers and sister were glad when I suggested that I keep our mother in my home and that I be paid a salary from her income.

Next, the loud yes. Some people will not consider any other arrangement than having parents stay in a family-supervised situation. That yes may come from the parents who feel that they would rather die than live anyplace other than their own home; or it may be from you or other members of your family who would consider it a disgrace to have someone else take care of your parents.

> As my mother grew older she made one point very clear: "I want to die in my own home." We thought she was saying that she would never live in a nursing home. However, as her physical health failed, we knew she had to have round-the-clock nursing care. We finally had to bring up the subject of a nursing home to her. To our surprise she quickly agreed that she needed to move out of her home to receive that care. When someone mentioned that she had said she wanted to die at home, her answer was, "I agreed to live in a nursing home. I didn't say I'd die there. I still plan to come home to die." So she's now content in a nursing home a few miles from the house she still calls home—and where she still plans to die.

It is worth the effort to evaluate even an obvious answer. Even if parents do remain in their home or another family home for the time being, is now a good time to look to the future and consider what their needs will be next year? Are there changes you can make now that will help make necessary changes later?

Second Floor: Board and Care Homes

The next level of possible care for your parents is a home, but not the home of a family member. This is perhaps one of the oldest resources available for elderly people who cannot live in their own or family member's homes. A few decades ago most towns of any size had a rooming house. A rooming house was a private home, often operated by a widow. Traveling salesmen were the main customers. But often older people who had no family would live in rooming houses for years. In recent years the rooming house has come back as a board and care home for elderly people.

A board and care home is often a private house—though sometimes it can be a small hotel remodeled for elderly people. It offers no medical care and few (if any) social services. It is a place to live, with meals provided.

Though board and care homes are available in most communities, they are not highly visible. Seldom are they in the Yellow Pages. They have no big signs out front and no large parking lots. They are homes. That hominess, in fact, is their main attraction for those who need their services.

Third Floor: Assisted Living

Assisted living facilities are for people who cannot maintain their own home but who do not need the full care of a nursing home. They range from the very luxurious retirement communities in the most expensive parts of the country to modest mobile-home parks that also provide some personal care. In fact, the great variety of assisted living facilities available can be confusing for those who must make decisions for their family members. But that variety means you'll likely find a facility to meet the exact needs of your family.

Fourth Floor: Nursing Homes

Nursing homes provide the maximum care needed for their residents. That care may be for those who are able to walk, dress themselves and take care of other personal needs. It may also be for those who are bedfast and totally dependent on others for all their needs. Many nursing homes also have sections for those who need only assisted-living help. As one's needs fluctuate, the resident may move from one section to another in the same institution to receive the proper care.

There are a great variety of nursing homes. Some are private businesses operated on a for-profit basis. Others are owned and managed by churches and other charity groups. Some are operated by city or county governments.

The chief advantages of nursing homes is 24-hour-a-day nursing care and a variety of social and therapeutic services. The disadvantages to many include the institutional atmosphere, and the large day rooms and halls often filled with silent people in wheelchairs. (It is a simple matter of financial math that the more services offered by a facility, the more people they must have to cover the cost of the extra care.)

How You Make Your Choice

The choice of care you select should not be made based on the title used by the facility. For purposes of evaluation I have divided the levels of care into four categories. But these levels of care do not have clear boundaries. There is a gradual blend from one to the other. Chances are, your loved one will not fit neatly into some prescribed definition.

73

Also many facilities for elderly people have names that do not actually describe their services. One board and care home that I visit regularly is called a retirement home. It is greatly different from the retirement communities that dot Arizona. Some places that do not offer nursing services are called nursing homes. This ambiguity in the names on the letterhead is not an attempt to conceal anything. Many of the businesses were started long ago before the industry developed the specializations available today. Others just picked a name that they thought sounded comforting.

Recognize that each facility will define itself by the residents it accepts. Some of the rules for admission may seem arbitrary to you.

> We found the perfect place for Mom. It was clean and comfortable. The staff was friendly and helpful. It was convenient and affordable. But the home had a rule that they would accept only people who were confined to wheelchairs. Mom was ninety-three but she didn't need and would not consider a wheelchair. So we had to find another place.

Your parents' health is not the only consideration as you determine the level of care that they need. Many people who live in their own home with families or in board and care homes are in much worse physical and/or mental health than those in nursing homes. On the other hand, sometimes people who are in reasonably good health must be in a nursing home because they do not have anyone who can take care of them anywhere else.

> My doctor, my pastor, my neighbors, even her sisters, have told me that I should put my wife in a nursing home. They all explain that it is for her good as well as mine I own. I agree with everything they say. But I won't do it,

and if you were in my situation, you wouldn't do it either. And you had better be careful about telling me what to do, because you don't know whether or not you will ever face the same situation. It's not easy.

At other times elderly people have attitudes that keep them out of any kind of home other than their own. Many have gone through difficulties in their lives by sheer determination. They have learned a way to cope with problems in life and they are not about to change just because they grew old.

My parents were strong-willed people and very self-reliant. They thought that they could go from complete independence to vegetable/dead without all those worrisome, interim steps. In actuality, it almost worked that way for them.

Mildred is so crippled that she can hardly walk. Sometimes it takes her fifteen minutes to walk the short distance to the bathroom. Yet she goes to church every Sunday, does her own shopping and visits family members. If you ask her why she doesn't go to a nursing home, or at least stay at home, she answers, "I'd hurt just as much if I were in a nursing home or if I sat around my own house. So why not go ahead and do something?"

Your choice of the level of care available for your parents will also be influenced by that important question: Who pays the bill? Rules made by those who operate insurance companies and provide public assistance funds are a final authority. Often people are required to use more expense care than they actually need because of the regulations of those who pay the bill. You need to know what those rules are before you search for a place for your parents. Do not waste valuable time looking at places that would not be acceptable by your insurance company or any public aid that your parents might be eligible to receive.

What About Finances?
The big question is, "What will this care cost?"

It is impossible here to give exact costs for caring for elderly people. You will find a wide range of rates for the many facilities in your own community. Nationwide the range of prices for care will even be greater. And prices everywhere will rise as the years go by.

In the meantime, however, consider the sources of money available to pay for your parents' care. About forty-five percent of all people in nursing homes pay for their own care—or it is paid by their families. To make a wise decision for your parents you will need to have full knowledge of their financial status. Begin by finding out their net worth. Is their money in stable investments, or will its value go up and down with real-estate prices, stock markets, or other places of investments? What is their monthly income from pensions, Social Security, and investments? Again, is this a fixed income or will it include cost-of-living adjustments? How much will investment income be affected by changes in interest rates?

The average stay in a nursing home is three years. That does not mean that the average person goes home after three years; it means he or she only lives that long. Still, three years is only an average. Some people live in nursing homes for fifteen to twenty years. Many people have commented, "If I knew exactly how long I was going to live, it would be a lot easier to plan my finances."

If you and other members of the family are going to pay the bill, you need to do the same evaluation about the dependability of your own income(s). What happens if you and others make commitments to pay the monthly fees for your parents, and then you have a big change in your financial circumstances? You may have a job change, major medical expenses, or other unplanned money drains. You cannot plan for every emergency, but you should have a Plan B in case a problem develops in Plan A.

About half of all nursing home care was paid by Medicaid and Medicare in 1991. These programs are always subject to political changes. Make sure you check with local governmental offices to know exactly what benefits your parents may receive and what the conditions are.

Approximately three percent of all nursing-home care is covered by insurance purchased for that purpose. Insurance especially designed to cover nursing-home care was introduced in the early seventies. Although it took a while for the industry to establish policies that included all variables, a number of reputable companies now have policies for people who plan to provide for their own expenses if and when they need to live in a nursing home.

The basic policy is simple: For an annual fee you have coverage for one year, but you are guaranteed that the policy is renewable. If you buy the policy at a young age, say 50, the premium will be lower, and will not increase as you grow older. (There may be exceptions to that rule; check them out.) If you buy the policy while you are in good health, you are also guaranteed insurability for the rest of your life.

Such a policy covers a set daily fee for nursing-home care. The daily rate you select helps to determine the cost of the insurance. You can also choose to buy a policy that will provide for two years, three years, or for the rest of your life in the nursing home. After you have been in the home for three months you stop paying premiums.

You can buy a variety of riders for a policy. One rider gives the policy a cash value and a return to your estate if you do not use it in a nursing home. Other riders will increase the amount paid per day for care.

Some policies will allow you to be paid partial benefits if you stay in a board and care home rather than a nursing home. The company must approve your living in a nursing home according to their requirements and the verification by a doctor.

Our parents made it easy for us to help them when they could not longer live at home. They had bought nursing-home insurance some years ago. The insurance policy gave us the freedom to find a good home for both Mom and Dad. Of all the planning we did together as a family, that was the most important decision.

You Need One Room

You need one room for one person—perhaps two. The number of options you have will depend on the size of your community. But even in a small city you can easily have more than a hundred facilities that could provide that one room for your family.

The sheer number of possibilities may seem like one more problem for you. Don't despair. I have spoken with many people in your situation. Their dining-room tables are covered with brochures from numerous care facilities and with pamphlets from a wide variety of agencies that provide help for the aged. One advantage you have is that all of the places available to you are businesses in one way or another. They want your business— without it they couldn't keep their doors open. The number of places available to you increases your chances of finding a good home for your parents at a price that you can afford. And while competition makes for better service at better prices, it also requires you to be more responsible for your decision.

We thought we had made good plans for our parents

when they needed to go to a nursing home. But now that we've gone through the experience we realize that our plans did not cover all the details that we have now seen are necessary.

Keep your own mental health in good order by appreciating the number of places available to you. The time you need to sort through all the possibilities is a good problem and worth the effort. If you need to move your parents several times (which happens often) each move will cause them and you to go through another adjustment period and can also add to your expenses.

Aunt Irma went through four nursing homes in five months after she had to leave her own apartment. She caused a lot of problems at each place After that awful start we found a place where she has stayed for over eleven years with few complaints. I'm not sure if the first four bad experiences were necessary for her to make the adjustments and accept the fact that she had to live in a nursing home, or if she would have been content had we chosen the last place first. Anyway it is a great relief to have her willingly stay in one place.

It's Time to Collect the Literature
Ask yourself the following questions:

1. Do I know who (individual or group) will make the decision regarding where my parents will live?
2. Do I know who will be able to support the decision that will be made?
3. Do I know what role my parents will have in making that decision?
4. Do I know that my parents will need to accept certain parts of the decision even though they may not like it?

5. Do I know what locality will be the best place for my parents to live?
6. Do I know what kind of care my parents need?
7. Do I know how much my parents (or whoever will be paying the bill) can spend per month for a place to stay?
8. Am I aware how long they (or we) can continue to pay that much for their care?

When you have said yes to these questions, you are ready to get out the Yellow Pages, read the brochures, and hit the streets to start looking at real places.

— 5 —
Level One:
Home Care

Taking care of elderly people in the family home is a part of the- way-it-has-always-been. Many families were, and a few still are, always together. In the Illinois community where I grew up, I know a family that has moved back and forth between two houses, which are only a short distance from each other, for five generations. The older generation is always cared for by the younger ones. It appears that the sixth generation will continue the tradition.

In many large cities the same process has often happened. The parents would live in one flat. When their child married they would move into the flat upstairs. The next generation would need their own home about the same time that the grandparents could share a flat with the middle generation. No one left home—not the younger generation when they married, not the older generation when they could no longer care for themselves.

Aging Parents

Some families that have moved from community to community, or state to state, still have maintained a way for the generations never to be divided.

We never had to make a decision about Mother living with us because we had always lived with her. In our fifty-three years of marriage, my husband and I have always lived in the same house with my mother. At first we lived with her. Then I guess she started living with us when we retired and moved to Arizona. It didn't make any difference; that's just the way we did things.

For most families, the decision is not that easy. The mobility of people and jobs, smaller homes, and a greater number of people living longer than before have combined to make it more difficult for elderly to have their parents live with them.

There is another complication. At the same time when the older generation is living longer, their grandchildren are remaining in the homes of their parents longer—and are frequently returning to their parental homes, sometimes bringing still another younger generation with them. I visited the home of an elderly man in the congregation I serve as pastor soon after our third and last child left home. The man saw my sadness and asked about it. I explained that our last child had moved away. He replied, "Don't count on it. They come back and they bring more with them!"

A typical couple in their upper middle ages today may find themselves:

a) with a smaller home than they have had before;
b) parents who want to live with them;
c) children and/or grandchildren that want to live with them;
d) all of the above. They may seriously hope for
e) a job offer in South America.

5 • Level One: Home Care

In today's world there is no typical situation, no one model for the proper way to care for aging parents. While there is a great increase in the number of facilities available to care for elderly people, home care is still the first option for most families. Sometimes this means their parents will move in with their children. Sometimes the younger generation will move into their parents' home. Occasionally they find a different house to accommodate the two generations.

You can benefit from knowing the experiences of others who have made the same decisions you are now facing. At the same time, you will have unique needs. What was a good solution for one of your friends might be a disaster for your family. A solution that was a failure for someone else might be the best thing that ever happened to your family.

> When my father died and Mom was alone, I expected her to want to live with us because all of my friends had told me their parents insisted on remaining with a member of the family. I knew it wouldn't work, because my wife and mother had never liked each other. I was surprised that my mother didn't want to live with us. She wanted to be in a place where someone would wait on her twenty-four hours a day. Dad had always babied her—and she expected that kind of care. She knew she wouldn't get it at my house.

The first question to consider is: Can my parents live with someone in the family—or can someone in the family live with them?

Who Will Be the Care Giver?
The primary question is not about the house, rather it is about the one who takes care of the house. The important fact to face is that when parents cannot live alone, it is rarely a building that is causing the problems. Instead it is the fact

that your parents need help in facing their changing conditions. They need a care giver. Note the change in terminology. A decade ago we talked about caretakers. There is a big difference between one who takes care of another and one who gives care to another. It's not just a change in words, but a change in attitudes. At all levels of physical and emotional need, people need someone to give them care. Being a caretaker is a burden. Being a care giver is a responsibility and a privilege.

> I know it sounds trite to say this, but I never understood how my parents took care of me until I took care of them. Like every other child I just accepted all that they gave me. But when it was my turn to help them they did not make that assumption. They felt that I was being forced to provide for them. We both had to work through the problem and understand that I was helping them because I wanted to.

The Nominee Is You

If you are thinking about having your parents move into your home— or if you are thinking about moving into theirs—then you are considering being the primary care giver. You need to evaluate your own ability and availability before you take on such a responsibility. (Although you may have been the primary decision maker regarding where your parents would live, that does not automatically make you the primary care giver or vice versa.

Being a care giver is an occupation for many people. It takes the energy, the time, and the abilities that are required for a full-time job. In addition, many professional care givers have had special education and on-the-job training for their work. Even though you are not applying for a career in care giving, trust me: you *will* be working at the job.

If your first question to yourself is, "Am I willing to take

5 • Level One: Home Care

care of my parents?" you'll probably put unnecessary guilt on yourself from the very beginning. You obviously do care about your parents or you would not be considering this position. You want your parents to have the best care possible. So now you must simply decide whether you are qualified for the job. If you have doubts about your ability to be objective, discuss some of the following issues with other members of your family, clergy, or someone who can help you understand yourself better as you make this important decision.

1. Can you do the physical work required of care givers? Are your parents especially heavy, or do they have other physical conditions that would require strength beyond that which you have? Could you endanger your parents by offering to do things that you would not be able to do? You will not be doing your parents a favor if you cause yourself physical or emotional problems in an attempt to help them in their problems. You may be better off paying someone to do what you cannot do. If you have health problems, you may want to include your doctor in this part of the decision.

2. Are you emotionally equipped for care giving? You will be working with your parents, not patients. Can you use the voice of authority to make your parents take medicine, do the necessary exercise, care for themselves as much as possible? Can you change a parent's diaper? Can you give your father or mother a bath and yet maintain their dignity—as well as your own?

> I love my mother, but I'm sorry to say there are times when I don't like her. If she lived in my home we would have disagreements all the time. The staff at the board and care home where she stays tells her to do things and there's no problem. She does what she is told to do. If I told her to do the same things, we'd have a major problem. Now when I come to visit her, there is no hassle. She

loves for me to come, and we have a good time.

Some people do these things with a sense of joy. They accept the fact that their parents need help and they would rather give the help themselves than have it done by strangers. Others cannot accept the change in roles. You will have to decide for yourself.

> There's no way I could pay someone to take care of my mother. I want to do it. I can't imagine myself going to visit her in some kind of a home and seeing someone else feed her or help her go to the bathroom. I don't take care of her because I have to do it. I want to.

You need also to recognize that you have years of emotional history with your parents. That history gives you the love for them, and their love for you, that makes you care about them now. But that history also includes some negative feelings. If you were working in a nursing home and taking care of someone else's parents, you could listen to their criticisms and not be affected by them. But when those criticisms come from your parents, they may dredge up memories long forgotten.

Your emotional history may make you want to be with your parents, but it may also make it difficult for you to care for them. Only you can sort that out. Ultimately, you must understand and accept the fact that being a son or daughter is more important than being a person who provides personal service. Your relationship with your parents makes your service more meaningful to them than that of a stranger. But it may also make it more difficult for both you and them.

> It turned out to be a good thing for my husband and me when my mother came to live with us. My husband is on

5 • Level One: Home Care

disability because of a series of strokes. I felt better going to work because I knew my husband felt needed at home as he helped take care of Mom. She also enjoyed "mothering" him and had a sense of being needed.

We call ourselves the three monkeys. My mother has a hearing problem, so she can hear no evil. My husband has a speaking problem due to the strokes, so he can speak no evil. I have cataracts, so I can see no evil. We need each other.

3. Do you have the ability to do the work? Each of us has special skills that we can use in our work and in our personal lives. But we also lack certain skills. Sometimes we don't know our weak areas until we try doing what we have not done before. For example, I have heard people imply that anyone could be a waitress: "If I have to, I'll get a job in a restaurant." But it's not the simple. A good waitress has very special skills. Those who don't have those skills don't last at the job. You are not automatically qualified to be the care giver just because you are a daughter or son.

Caring for elderly people requires patience, cheerfulness, cleanliness, and devotion to detail. It requires living on a rigid schedule of medications and treatments. It requires the ability to repeat the same functions over and over again; then over and over again. It requires the ability to listen and to speak—in that order.

I welcomed the idea of staying home and taking care of Dad. No more early-morning alarm clocks. No more rushed breakfasts. No more long rides to work. No more office gossip. No more cash layout for office clothes and lunch. But it didn't work that way. Within two weeks I had cabin fever. I missed getting dressed up. I couldn't handle daytime TV. I needed the challenge of work. Then I realized that all I had needed was a vacation—not a career change. You may need someone else to evaluate your ability to do the work of providing for your parents; choose someone who does not have a vested interest in the decision. Do not feel guilty about what you honestly cannot do. You want your parents to have the best care possible.

Your love for your parents is your main qualification for the job. In a study of day care for children, the attention was focused on the training and skill of the staff and the safety and attractiveness of the facility. However, the conclusion was that those things were not the most important. The report concluded that in caring for children nothing can replace the irrational love of parents and grandparents. The same may be said about the love of children and grandchildren for elderly people. However the question remains: Does your love require that you give the care yourself, or that you provide it through others?

4. Do you have the time to take care of your parents? You may feel that you are required to find the time—and that may be true. However, you need to understand that when you agree to add something to your schedule, you will also need to cut something out. If you were to be the primary care giver for your parents, what would you eliminate from your present schedule in order to find the time needed for your extra work?

Will you take time away from other family members? Do they understand that? Do they interpret that sacrifice of time as their way of helping people who are also important to them? Instead of spending a weekend away with your spouse, you may be spending that time with your parents. Do you both understand that? Will you take time that is now given to children or grandchildren? Will they resent that loss of your time? Will *you* resent it? These issues will not be the only factors to consider as you make your decision, but you need to address them and discuss them with others who are involved.

> After our children left home, my mother came to live with us. Our youngest daughter was jealous. Her grandmother now had her room, her place at the family table, and most of all, her parents' care and attention. All of us, perhaps even our daughter, were surprised at the reaction. But we had to face it. The issue was not resolved until our daughter got married.

If you are employed, will your job of taking care of your parents interfere with the job for which you are paid? Will it interfere with your spouse's job? From a practical point of view, could you make more money at your present job and pay for someone to care for your parents—even in your home?

5. If you don't take the job, who will? This is a dangerous question, but it must be asked. If you agree to care for your parents only because that seems to be the only choice, you are facing problems. You could feel resentment because the task was forced on you. You might not be able to do the job. Or your own situation in life could change, making care giving impossible. For your parents' security as well as your own, you need a Plan B. And as you make your decision, consider the possibility that Plan B might be better than Plan A.

If you don't take your parents into your home, would you be jealous or unhappy if they went to the home of some other family member? Do not let your parents be the victims of family conflicts.

> I worked with a family of three daughters and two elderly parents. The parents had health problems and some financial difficulties. Every conversation started with one sister announcing what she wanted done. From then on the discussion would be about what that sister wanted rather than what the parents needed. What may have

been real love for her parents caused great difficulties for the entire family. That one sister made herself the problem—and prevented others from finding a solution that helped the parents.

If you are to become the primary care giver you need to know who made the choice: you? the care receiver? other members of the family? It is much easier if you can make the decision based on the issues discussed in this chapter. But your parents may assume that you will take care of them, even though you are not sure about it.

I had a bachelor uncle to whom I gave some special attention because no one else in the family did. He lived in Florida, so I would see him only every two or three years. One day I got a phone call from a hospital in his community. He had had a stroke and had given my name as his nearest relative. They strongly suggested I come to see him. My wife and I had some vacation time available so we decided to drive to Florida.

When we got to the hospital my uncle said, "You know, I've been thinking about it, Herb, and I think you are right. I had better come and live with you." My wife and I panicked because we had never considered the possibility. But we seemed to have no choice. He's been with us for three years now. And it has worked. He's a problem at times, but we are glad that he is with us.

If you feel you have been drafted to become the primary care by your parents or members of your family, you will start out with a built-in difficulty. Give yourself time to evaluate yourself and he situation. Accept the choice only if you can do it without resentment against those who picked you.

5 • Level One: Home Care

A Paid Care Giver

Often the simple solution to care for elderly parents is to employ a person to live in their home with them. A different version of the same solution is to have your parents live in your home but to hire someone to care for them. In some cases this might be a good solution.

If you want someone to care for your parents in their home, you need to recognize the difficulties of such a job. So equipped, you may be able to overcome some of the problems of such an arrangement.

> We tried hiring someone to come to our home to take care of Mom. It just didn't work. One would not show up for work without giving us a call. Several took the job to tide themselves over while they looked for other work and then quit without giving us notice. One thought of it as a "sitting" job and did nothing but sit.

> We thought our best choice was to hire someone to take care of Dad during the day. But it didn't work. Dad was too cantankerous. We interviewed and found good help, but none of them would put up with Dad's nasty disposition.

First, the job of taking care of an older person does not offer long term employment—at least it doesn't seem to. The elderly person might die, and the care giver is out of work. In a live-in care giver situation, the care giver will find herself (nearly all such care providers are women) without a home as well. She will need to find another position immediately. You can frankly discuss such a possibility and include some help in your job offer. Or you might agree to allow her to continue living in your parents' home for a specific length of time after your parents' death.

Next, live-in care givers need time off. It can too easily

become a twenty-four hour a day, seven day a week job. Members of the family will need to be available to fill in on certain evenings and days. Those times should not be changed except with advanced notice and the agreement of the care giver.

> When Mom died we had a problem because she had always taken care of Dad. We all thought Dad would go first. After a couple of failures we found the right lady to move into Dad's home and take care of him. She was wonderful. We helped her fix up a room with her own furniture. She had her own telephone in the room. But the job turned out to be too big for one person. Although she really needed the job and we liked her, Dad had to go into a board and care home.

The next concern is for you. Often a person looking for a live-in job is going through her own transition time. Maybe she has had a death in her family or gone through a divorce. As she makes the adjustments, she may find she wants more freedom than the job allows. So you start looking again.

The good side is that some live-in care givers become part of the family and genuinely care for the people for whom they work. If you find that situation, don't wait until Thanksgiving Day to express your appreciation.

The Other Nominees Are

As you consider yourself as the possible care giver for your parents, be aware that other members of the family may also be thinking that they should take care of your parents. If you have brothers and sisters consider each of them. In some cases in-laws (even former in-laws) may have close attachments to your parents and might want to help provide for their care. In other situations, one of your parents' brothers or sisters might have both the ability and the desire to help.

5 • Level One: Home Care

We knew Mom could no longer live alone. But the last person we would have asked to move in to help her was the youngest brother. The entire family had spoiled him. He couldn't cook. He thought cleaning up had something to do with the stock market. But suddenly he became aware of all the care Mom had given him. He insisted on moving in to take care of her. We thought that it would last for a few months—at best. But he learned to take care of a home. We can't believe how well he has provided for Mom. And he's happy about it!

The idea of having a big family conference to discuss the care of your parents sounds great, but it is often difficult to get everyone together at the same time. One alternative is to circulate a round robin letter. To get the letter started, make a list of all members of the family who need to be included. Write your evaluation of the situation and offer what you can do to help your parents. Send your letter to the first person on the list. Then ask each of the others to add their letter and mail the packet on to the next. This may take more time than you have available. But this is a family decision and even those who may not be able to be the primary care giver need to be aware of the needs and possible solutions.

Remember that whoever calls the meeting or starts the round robin letter is assuming a leadership role that may be seen by other members of the family as a way of volunteering. However, it is a responsibility that someone has to take. You need to know the dynamics of your family and how they do or do not participate in decision making. Don't let other family problems become a part of this issue. The best way to do that is to acknowledge the other problems and to ask everyone to put them aside for the sake of your parents.

Can the Job Be Shared?

One of the dangers of being the primary care giver for elderly people is that one becomes the *only* care giver. You and other members of your family may hesitate to have your parents live with you because you fear that you will become totally responsible for them. In some cases that does happen. But it need not.

The person who takes the primary care giver position needs to know what additional support is available. If one person in the family lives with the parents, other members can provide time or money to help not only the parents but also the care giver. Community agencies also provide help for elderly people who remain in private homes. Each state, city, and county has its own system. Do not depend on what you have learned from friends and neighbors to know what is available. Ask your doctor or the social services department of your hospital for suggestions.

A Family Team

Let's look at several possibilities of how a family can have one primary care giver for elderly parents and how others can be supportive.

When family members all live near each other. The parents could live with one of their children. The son or daughter with whom they live would be the primary care giver. However, that person may work outside the home and need to be gone every day. Another son or daughter, who has different working hours or is not employed, could remain with the parents while the primary care giver is at work. Perhaps several of the older people's children, and even grandchildren, could be in on the arrangement. This way the parents see more members of the family regularly. The primary care giver can continue his/her own life with some free time.

If the parents are physically able they may live in one of their children's homes, but spend the day hours in the home of another. Or they may spend weekends visiting other members of the family, so the primary care giver has some free time.

The parents may live with one of their children, but other children become responsible for certain tasks. One takes care of the finances. Another sees to it that the parents can visit the doctor, dentist, go shopping, and attend church. One may take care of laundry, or bring in meals (especially if the parents have special dietary needs).

When members of the family live far from each other. Brothers and sisters who live miles from each other cannot provide the day by day help that the primary care giver often needs. But they can be of help. Regular phone calls and letters help the parents keep alert and feel more content. Those who live away can come to stay with the parents while the primary care giver takes a vacation or goes on a business trip. Those who live away can invite parents (and provide transportation if necessary) to visit.

Each family will need to figure out its own way of dividing financial responsibilities. The simple way is to total the costs and divide by the number of children—but rarely will it work as easily as that. Those who are providing more time and energy should provide less money. Other considerations such as the individual financial situation of each family member must be considered.

If the parents go to live in the home of one of the children, the others should be aware of the extra expenses for that member of the family. If the parents have a monthly income, it should be used to help cover those expenses. If not, other members of the family can share the financial needs.

Community Resources

The primary care giver may also be able to receive a variety of help from the community. Since each area has its own special resources, it is impossible to list the exact help you can expect where you live. In addition, the availability of public help for elderly people can increase or decrease on short notice. The good news is that because more people are living longer, there is an increased interest in help for the elderly. Politicians and business people are aware of the votes and the economic boost when businesses and services are offered for the elderly. At the same time, many programs are losing public funding and insurance companies are becoming more restrictive in the needs that they cover.

In general, most communities offer more help to families than is generally known. It's worth the effort to check out your area to see what resources are available. Start your search by knowing what you need. What help do you need to be able to keep your parents in your or their home?

If your parents need regular medical attention, you may be able to have a home care nurse visit them regularly. The social services department of a hospital will know what resources are available and how they are financed. In today's world few people stay in a hospital for long periods of time. Instead they are transferred to a nursing home that serves as a halfway house between home and hospital, or they are sent home when medical and therapy can be provide there. The hospital will provide names of agencies and phone number to help you find out what kind of support you can have at home. In some cases, they will provide help with house cleaning and food preparation. Others may arrange regular visits by Licensed Practical Nurses (LPNs) to help bathe elderly people.

Some communities also have respite homes to provide day care for elderly people. These homes may be run by churches, nursing homes, or government programs. They function very much like a day care center for children. Elderly people may stay several hours a day, several days a week. The center provides activities, a meal, and social contact.

5 • Level One: Home Care

We were ready to put Mom in a nursing home when we found the respite center. At first she objected loudly. But when she faced the choice of giving up her home permanently or going to the center three days a week, she took the respite care. Now she loves it. She brings home the crafts she makes. She has something to talk about. And the other day she even admitted that they served her a good lunch.

If you live in a smaller community that does not have day care for adults, you might consider contacting other people in your situation and helping one another. For example, some churches offer a "Mother's Day Out," during which moms bring their children to the church. They take turns staying with the children while the others go out to lunch, shopping, or a movie. The same system could work for elderly people. You might use a church facility or one of your homes. You would have some free time, plus your parents would have contact with other people. You might also benefit from becoming part of a good support group with others who are also caring for their parents.

Some communities also provide free, or very inexpensive, transportation for elderly people. Vans designed to help people in wheelchairs will pick up people at their homes, take them to where they want to go, and bring them back. Reservations often have to be made in advance, and it is not taxi service. While the riders may have to wait a while, at least they have something to wait for.

Here is another resource that can be helpful to you if you decide to keep your parents in your home: Some nursing homes will keep people for short periods of time. Your parents might live with you, but you could arrange for them to be in a nursing home for a weekend, or for several weeks while you take a vacation—or stay home by yourself. Most elderly people are not thrilled with this service, but they may see that you also need a vacation time, or you may have another physical or personal need that requires your attention for a while. This may also expose your parents to life in a nursing home and help them prepare for a permanent change later. To be honest, we must also admit that it may anger them and make them vow never to go live in a nursing home. But that's a chance you, and they, may have to take.

> My mother lived with us, but she made it easy for us because she knew my husband and I needed time alone. She never made us feel guilty when we needed to be with other members of the family, go on a business trip, or take a vacation. She would insist on spending that time in a nursing home. (She was able to pay her own expenses for the time in a nursing home, which also made it easier for us and made her feel she was giving something to us.) It was a vacation for her too, and we all enjoyed each other more when we were all home again.

Many churches have a program called Stephen Ministry. Members of the congregation are trained to be care givers to people in a great variety of needs. If your parents live in your home, you might request a Stephen Minister to be assigned to them. Some congregations provide this service even for those who are not members. Stephen Ministers do not function as "gofers," but they serve by listening and caring.

> My mother looks forward to the weekly visit from her Stephen Minister. Even though Mom is not an outgoing person—and never liked to be in large groups—that one-on-one visit is important to her. She feels connected with her church again, even though she can't attend.

An emergency call service is also available for elderly

5 • Level One: Home Care

people who live alone or who live with family but must be alone at certain times. It is a simple process: You may lease a small device to be worn around the neck at all times. If a subscriber to the service has an emergency, he or she may push a button on the device and an alarm is sounded. This is a nationwide service, so different communities have different arrangements. In large areas the national company contracts with local hospitals to take the emergency calls. In smaller communities the call is taken by a central office that in turn calls a local emergency service. Keep in mind that this is a private business, not a public health service. Check out the history of the company you are considering for this service through local agencies for the elderly. Also, there are two charges: one for the lease of the equipment— generally from a local hospital—and one for the monthly monitoring service. When this service works properly it gives families of elderly people a good back up system. And although the emergency call service may be expensive, it is less expensive than other alternatives for 24-hour-a-day protection.

To find out more about these programs, and other help in your community, look in your phone book for a Council on Aging under state, county, or city government. Your community many have different titles for their services. Search both the Yellow Pages and the listing of government agencies. Look for items such as "Senior Awareness Program" and other listings under "Senior," "Elderly" or "Aged." Also watch your newspaper for workshops provided for care givers in the community. Such workshops are often sponsored by church and public health groups. By attending you not only will discover what is available in your area, you can meet other people who share your concerns.

Finally, contact your local branch of the American Association of Retired Persons. If they are not listed in your phone book, write to: AARP, 1909 K Street N.W., Washington,

D.C. 20049. They can give you up-to-date information on resources available to you in your community.

The House That Is Home

Our attention has been on the people who care rather than the building that gives shelter. As important as the people are, the condition of the house where you live must also be considered. You and other members of your family may have the best intentions and the deepest love for your parents; that does not mean it would always be best for your parents to live with you. You must consider whether or not they need more care than you can provide—that's for later chapters. But you must also consider whether it even is possible, or advisable, for your parents to live in a private home.

Let's take an objective look at the house you are considering as a home for you and your parents. In most cases, it is the home where you or they now live. In a few cases, it will be a home bought or rented for that purpose. If it is your or their present home, remember that you and they have a lot of emotional investment in that real estate. That emotional investment may override the practical disadvantages of the house. So dress up in whatever it takes to make you feel as logical as possible and take a walk around the house and neighborhood under consideration.

First, look at the neighborhood. Is it a good, safe area? Do you have adequate (why not go for excellent) police, fire, and emergency protection? How far are you from urgent-care services? In the last five years has this house been blocked from public access by floods, snow, or ice? How serious do you consider the possibility of earthquakes, forest fires, or mudslides? None of these issues should have a major role in your final decision; however, each of them adds a plus or minus point that must be included in your final vote.

5 • Level One: Home Care

Now drive up to your house from the street. How close can you park to the front door? Would bad weather block access to the house? How many steps must you walk from where you get out of the car until you are in the house? Could a ramp be built to eliminate all the steps? If your home is an apartment, do you have elevator service? Are the elevators built for people in wheelchairs?

Let's go inside. Would your parents be able to live on one level of the house? An upstairs is not bad if your parents will not need to use it. In fact, two levels can offer more privacy for both you and your parents if both floors have bathrooms. A split-level house and a sunken living room are advertised features in many new homes today; they are hindrances in homes for the elderly.

What kind of floor coverings do you have? Carpets provide a softer landing if an elderly person falls, but they are difficult for people in wheelchairs; shag carpets are impossible. Tile floors are better for wheelchairs, but bad for those using crutches and canes. Throw rugs are out!

Borrow a wheelchair and ride around the house. Can you get down the halls? Into the bathroom? Lunch counters don't work for people sitting in a wheelchair. Would the kitchen allow an elderly person to get a drink, raid the refrigerator, heat a meal? Would your parents be able to take a bath or shower?

Does the house have smoke alarms and fire extinguishers? Are the phones within reach of an elderly person? Are there hazards such as pools, spas, sunken bathtubs?

How much furniture would need to be replaced? Are there chairs your parents could use? Are coffee tables, lamp cords or grandchildren's toys cluttering up the place and making it dangerous for elderly people? Would your parents need a different bed? If both of your parents are involved, do they need separate bedrooms because of different sleeping patterns?

Aging Parents

How easy is it to open doors in the house? Round door-knobs must have been invented by a young, healthy person who never carried anything more than a key chain. Those who have even a mild case of arthritis and who carry canes, groceries or oxygen tanks would prefer levers as door handles. Changing doorknobs can be one of the easiest and least expensive alterations to your house.

Does the home offer privacy for both you and your parents? Is there a place that either of you can have guests while the other continues normal at-home activities? Will there be disagreements over which TV program to watch? If you have more than one TV set, who gets the one with the VCR? If you or your parents listen to music, radio, or TV in your own rooms at your own volume, will everyone else hear it?

I started my writing career by taking a week's vacation each year in a small town far from anyone I knew, so I could write without interruptions. One year I was in an old rooming house in a small town in southern Georgia. All the other residents were elderly people. All week long I worked at my typewriter while trying to block out the sounds of a great variety of soap operas, game shows, country music, and commercials at full volume. But on Saturday night every TV set was tuned to Lawrence Welk. I felt like I was working in his orchestra pit. I handled Welk's "wunnerful" music for one night, but that was my limit. You will need to know yours!

So far you've looked at the house where your parents might live as it exists at the present time. What about it could be changed? You can change floor coverings, add a ramp and do some other modifications at a reasonable expense without changing the resale value of your home. However, to widen hallways, redo a bathroom for a handicapped person, or remove a sunken living room is a major remodeling job. Will it be worth the expense? If you have to sell the

5 • Level One: Home Care

home, most such modifications will not increase the value; some may decrease it.

Would it be worthwhile to make major changes in the house by making a separate living area with its own entrance, kitchen, and bathroom? Such an apartment may add to the value because it could have a variety of uses by a future owner. Check the zoning for your area before you make plans. Your neighborhood could be for single family dwellings only.

You may wish to consider purchasing ECHO (Elder Cottage Housing Opportunity) housing. ECHO housing is a portable dwelling that typically is placed as a free-standing unit in a back yard. It is not a mobile home but is built specifically for elderly and handicapped people. It becomes a private home for your parents, yet it is nearby where you can provide for their daily care. After it has served its purpose an ECHO unit may be sold and moved to another location. Again, you would need to be sure that such a unit would fit the zoning laws of your community. For more information about ECHO units write to: AARP, 1909 K Street N.W., Washington, D.C. 20049.

The House Rules
One of the main advantages for elderly people to remain in their own home or live in the home of one of their children is that they are more in charge of their lives. All homes for the aged operate with house rules—sometimes implied but most often clearly spelled out. Often the rules that are needed for a group of people living together are in opposition to the desires of some individuals; they would prefer to live by their own rules. On the other hand, some elderly people need the group rules. In a home away from their own home they would have to conform to ways that they would not in their own house. Consider some of the following to help you determine if your parents would lose something or gain

something if they left their own home.

1. At your home, you keep your own pets. A few institutions now allow pets, but most often they provide the animal. Some people are tightly connected to their own special pet. Giving up the pet could be a major tragedy.

> My sister talked me into getting rid of my dog. She made me worry about what would happen to Schaunzie if I had to go to the hospital or to a nursing home. She made me think I would be cruel to keep the dog, so I gave Schaunzie away. That was a year ago. I still miss him. And I think he misses me.

2. Today we live in a "No Smoking" world except in specially designated (often outside) areas and in our own homes. It may be a good idea for your parents to stop smoking, but could you enforce such a rule in your home or theirs?

3. No alcohol is allowed in most nursing home. Other retirement homes may let you make your own rules.

> Uncle Clay needed a gin and tonic every afternoon at four. It was as important to him as any other part of his daily routine—perhaps more important. When he went to a nursing home, I checked to see if I could provide the afternoon gin and tonic at least once in a while. The answer was no, and I was told that any attempt to sneak alcohol into the nursing home would cause serious problems for Uncle Clay. I think I was more disappointed than my uncle because I wanted to do something to help him. His change of surroundings, and Aunt Mina's death, helped him accept other changes. He forgot about his four o'clock appointment with a gin and tonic, and I learned to appreciate the rule.

4. Most nursing home menus give two choices: Take it or leave it. At home a person can have the kind of food that is familiar. When my father was in a hospital he told the doctor, "I think I'd get better if Edna cooked my meals," so the doctor sent him home and Mom prepared his meals. His health improved markedly. Still, the fact remains that nursing homes provide well-planned and nutritionally balanced meals. They can keep better count of calories and cholesterol than someone at home who has raid-the- fridge privileges.

5. Any facility that provides care for a number of people needs routines. There is a time to get up, a time for a bath, and a time to go to bed. Some people resent the routine and can function better on their own system. However others may need a routine to avoid sleeping late, napping all day and staying awake all night— and often keeping others awake too.

6. Most elderly people need some medication. Often they need to take pills up to eight times a day—and different medications at different times. Nursing care facilities can insure that the proper medications are given at the proper times. They can also make sure that the pills are actually swallowed in case the elderly person likes to resort to childhood games again. To help those who give medication at home, a special container can be bought at a drug store. The container has a variety of compartments. The pills are placed in the compartments that are labeled according to the time they are to be taken. This way the patient or the care giver does not have to open a variety of bottles—and it offers an easy way to see that the medications have been taken.

7. Health care facilities have requirements about personal hygiene. An occasional elderly person will resist at home that which is required without question in an institution.

The Answer for You

The majority of elderly and handicapped people still live by themselves or with members of their families. Many of them have devised creative ways to make the living arrangements possible. Many people try a variety of arrangements before they find one that works. Others go through a number of situations only to find that none of them works. Yet they have not wasted their time—nor has the effort been lost on their parents. By trying other methods that were not successful, some families have discovered that other institutions for elderly people are a great idea. After their unsuccessful attempts, everyone involved has a greater appreciation for professional help in a home for the elderly.

—6—
Level Two:
Board and Care Homes

This level offers you an opportunity to look at the great variety of possible homes for your parents that are not provided by your own family—and yet are not retirement communities or nursing homes. That variety will require some work on your part because you will need to find and check out the many places in your community that offer board and care services for elderly people. However, that variety also gives you a greater possibility of finding a place specifically tailored to your parents' needs.

First, let's define a board and care home so you will know what you are looking for—and what you are not looking for. The range of homes that are a part of this category fit into the space between a family home on one end and an assisted care or nursing home on the other.

The category *board and care homes* covers a wide assortment of facilities for elderly people, many of which will be called by different names. Some will be called boarding homes; the management offers nothing more than a room—and perhaps meals. (Many owners of board and care homes object to the title *boarding home*, because it fails to recognize the special care they give to elderly people.) Some are called adult care homes. I am using "board and care" in this chapter because I want to emphasize the two important features of these houses: a place to stay that offers special care.

The main difference between the homes in this category and those considered in the previous chapter is that board and care homes are businesses and, like all businesses, they have to make a profit to stay open. On the other hand, they are not nursing homes or retirement communities that provide a menu of medical and social services. In most cases this type of facility is used by people who can still provide some care for themselves, or by families that need a place for elderly parents to live, but who still want to—and are able to—be involved in some of the personal care of their parents.

Board and care homes are not as puvlicly visible as nursing homes and retirement communities. They may look like just another house in the neighborhood, like a small apartment complex, or once in a while like a small hotel or motel. They depend on word-of-mouth advertising. In some communities the owners of board and care homes form an association to provide a referral service and to do some joint advertising. These associations also have requirements for their members and provide a variety of inspections and training for management and staffs. It is likely that a doctor, nurse, or pastor will know the locations of board and care homes. You also my hear about them from your friends and neighbors who have elderly parents.

The congregation that I serve as pastor has about 40 shut in people. About 25% of them are in board and care homes.

6 • Level Two: Board and Care Homes

Ten years ago none were in this kind of a facility. It is one of the most rapidly expanding methods of care for the elderly.

Find Out What Is Available in Your Community
The board and care home is ideal for people who cannot remain in a family home but who do not need the full care of a nursing home. Yet there are many levels of care available in the general category of board and care homes.

> When I started my search for a place for my mother, I found that the board and care homes had one immediate advantage for me over the nursing homes. I wanted to meet with the management of the place where Mom might live. In the nursing homes all of the management people worked regular business hours—the same that I did. It was difficult for me to get an appointment with them. But the board and care homes were often owned or at least operated by people on the scene. I could visit them in the evenings or on the weekends.

Perhaps you know people who would take care of your parents in their home. The only differences between this kind of care and that discussed in the last chapter would be that your parents are living in a home of someone who is not a relative, and that you, or your parents, are paying for the services. To check out this possibility look for those who are already caring for an elderly person in their own family. Since their home and their schedule is already adjusted to taking care of the elderly, they might also take another person into their home. Or find someone who has a family home and whose children have moved away. They may need some income to maintain the larger home. They may want to have someone else in the house with them. Such an arrangement is a private deal. It can happen only if you know someone who might take care of your parents, or if you have a "matchmaker" in your circle of friends who knows your needs and knows someone who could help fill those needs. It may be a long shot, but it does happen.

Another possibility is that a number of elderly people (singles or couples) go in together and share a home. They may think of themselves as roommates and enjoy having "roomies" again. Or they can identify their arrangement as an old folks commune. The idea is simple: A number of people pool their resources. Their Social Security and retirement checks will go further if they rent a five- bedroom house than if each rented a one-bedroom place. Each still has her or his own bedroom, but they all share living and kitchen space.

But they can pool more than their money. One may be able to cook. Another still drives a car. One may do the laundry and another cleans. They may also pool their family resources—"My daughter will take us to the doctor"; "Your son takes care of repairs on our house"; "My family will bring in one meal a day for all of us, and your family pays the electric bill."

Such roommate arrangements may be planned by several elderly people or their families as an individual endeavor. More often they are arranged by agencies that provide care for elderly people. This may be done through a local council on aging or other groups. Establishing such a communal house will take a lot of energy and planning. Details of what is expected of each person must be put on paper. The group will also need clear-cut policies to determine when one of its residents is no longer physically or mentally able to stay in the house. Having a church or other community group take care of the organization and supervision makes it easier for this method to work; however, it can be done by the individuals and families involved. Once the arrangement is established, those in charge should come up

6 • Level Two: Board and Care Homes

with a waiting list of prospective residents. If one person dies or moves away from the home, it would upset the financial balance. Preparations must be made for those possibilities by having reserve funds and a list of potential new residents.

Another possibility is to find a communal house that is already operational and has some kind of management. A woman in the congregation I serve has willed her five-bedroom home to our parish. Upon her death, we will use the home to provide housing for members who cannot live with their families and who do not yet need the services of a nursing home. Many churches operate such home collectives through agencies of their denomination.

> When my mother was still in good health and lived in her own home she always told us that if she needed to go to a home, she wanted it to be the one operated by our church about 120 miles from where she lived. Even though it was a distance away, she felt an ownership in the home. Her ladies group at church had given money and gifts to the home. She had visited there and she knew people there. Her identity with the place made the decision and the move easy for all of us.

The next level of a board and care home is a private home operated by the people who own it. Some people have accidently gotten into the board and care home business. They may have started with a member of their own family and decided it was as easy to take care of three elderly people as it is to care for one. Others may have agreed to take care of one elderly person for a month—and five years later still had that one person, plus four more.

> Ten years ago I worked in a nursing home and was frustrated because I could not care for people the way I

wanted. It seemed too impersonal to me. At the same time, my husband and I decided we wanted to stay in our large home after our childred moved away. So I quit work and found three elderly people through my church who needed a place to live. Since then we have added on to the house, and now we have ten full- time residents.

Many people have recognized that providing care for the elderly is an important service needed by many people. It is a valuable way to use one's time, resources, and abilities to make a living.

My husband wanted to retire early and write a novel. We have always enjoyed being with elderly people, so we supported ourselves by taking some older folks into our home. It has become a good business. We have bought a second house and are filled to capacity. He's still working on the novel, but we have found a good second career.

Note that often (perhaps not always) board and care homes are operated by people who have a mission in life. It's not just a way to make money. While they must charge for their services to stay in business, they truly want to help people. You may be looking for that attitude as you search for a place for your parents to live.

I am more comfortable with the idea that my mother must live with strangers because they don't seem like strangers. The people at the board and care home call me by my name. I can phone them and they phone me on matters that will help my mother.

The one-home business for board and care of elderly people can expand into a large business with many houses or to larger complex of rooms or apartments. You may see some facilities that you regard as nursing homes that are in reality board and care homes. It is not necessary for this book, or for you, to draw the line between which institution is a board and care home and which is a retirement or nursing home. Instead it is necessary for you to find out what place offers the best home for your parents.

Who Runs the Place?
The first time you go out to look at a place where your parents might live, the temptation will be to start by inspecting the room, the closet, and the bathroom. Those things are necessary, but they are not the highest priority.

The most important part of the facility where your parents will live is the people who run it.

Find out who is in charge of the place, or the part of the place, where your parents will live. If this is a one-house home and care facility, that person will be the owner. If it is a larger business the owner may be a business person who is remote from the day-by- day events in the home. In that case, find out who is in charge of the routine operation of the home; that person will set the tone for other employees and for the residents. It is important that both you and your parents like that person.

Getting acquainted with the person in charge is a two-way experience: you get acquainted with the management and the management gets acquainted with you. If that person gives you a good sales pitch when you first meet, but does not continue to provide the services promised, you will regret having your parents in that home. On the other hand, if you do not express all of your concerns about your parents' needs and later make demands that were not a part of your agreement, the management will regard you as a fault-finding, trouble-making person and be sorry that your parents are in their home. It is important that you be open about all of your parents' negative characteristics and about their physical and mental condition. You'll want to know what you should expect from this relationship. The managers of the home feel the same way.

> Clara is a problem in our home because she is a complainer. Nothing pleases her. But I am comfortable with having her here because her children told me that she would not be satisfied in my home—at least that she had never been satisfied with much in her life. Since I know that her children not only understand but even appreciate me for enduring the griping; she is no problem for me. I don't think it is my job to change her personality. When her children visit they stay as long as they can and always give me a special "thank you" when they leave.

Be open with the person in charge of the home. Explain what your major requirements are. Listen to what that person wants to offer. Some will emphasize the cleanliness of the building and the residents. Others will start with safety. Others will talk about food and exercise. Others will show a concern for the personal dignity of elderly people and their privacy. Some will show a sense of humor. Some will know every person in the home by name and by personality. All of these things are important. But some will be more important than others. You will need to know what is best for your parents—and for you.

> I was upset when the manager of the home phoned and said Mother had fallen. She had to have three stitches on her forehead because she had hit a chair as she went down. Her arm also had a bad bruise.
> The manager explained that my mother wanted to walk all the time. We knew that. We had moved her because the previous home was not able to keep her inside, and we were worried that she would walk too far

and not find her way back. The manager explained, "We had to make a decision between restraining her to protect her or to let her walk. We considered the impact of both and decided to let her walk. That's why she fell."

I felt bad about my mother's pain because of the fall. But I knew they had made the right choice for Mom. I assured the person who made the decision that I agreed with it. I realized how difficult it would have been for me if my mother were living in my home and I had to make those decisions. I appreciate the close contact I have with the person who cares for her.

People who work in homes for the elderly must make many decisions regarding their care. The management will set the priorities for those decisions. Just as in school some students do better in an open classroom atmosphere while others do better in a structured environment, so also elderly people have different needs. If your parents are able to be in a board and care home, they are able to express their needs. You will need to be aware if there is a conflict between what you think your parents need and what they think they need. The management of the home cannot be caught in a disagreement between you and your parents. No home can be the perfect place for every elderly person. Likewise, every elderly person is not a perfect candidate for every board and care home.

Aunt Emma went through four homes in six months. She demanded to leave one, was obnoxious enough to get kicked out of another, and faked a suicide attempt to escape the third. Now she has been in the same place for over eleven years. And she is content. It is a Jewish home, and—I'm sorry to say—Aunt Emma has strong anti-Jewish feelings. For the first six months in the home she would ask visitors to bring her bacon or ham, food she had had

115

no particular need for before. But she responded to the kind care she received and has settled down to stay— even without pork on her menu.

In an individual board and care home, one person will set the tone for all who live and work there. However, in larger facilities there will be a variety of people in charge on different shifts and different days. The attitudes and personalities of those people will be very important for the well-being of your parents. Visit the home at different times to see if the emotional atmosphere changes with the people on duty.

While those in charge of a facility set the tone for all who work there, others who work there are also important. The people who cook the food, make the beds, mow the yard and clean the rooms may seem like hired help, but they will have daily contact with those who live in the home. Watch how the people who work there treat those who live there.

Dad was depressed when he went into the home after Mom had died. He had planned to die first and was angry about the situation. At first he refused to talk to anyone. He just pouted. But I discovered that the lady who changed his bed and brought fresh towels had lived in England while her husband was in the military. I told her Dad had traveled in England. They had something to talk about. Then I noticed the young man who mopped floors. He was working for minimum wage I am sure. But he knew all the residents by their names. He kidded with them. He also helped Dad re-enter the social world.

While visiting the home, pay attention to those who already live there. Talk to the residents. Are they your parents' kind of people? Do they have about the same degree of abilities as your parents? In a smaller home, there is less variety. Will your parents regard the others as too quiet and stand-offish? Or will they think the other residents are too talkative and nosey? Imagine your parents sitting at the dining room table in the home. Then see them in a living room or out on porch. Ask yourself, "What's wrong with this picture?" Then ask, "What's right with this picture?"

What Do You Need? What Is Offered?

Your search for a place for your parents to live is not an effort to eliminate the bad places and find the good ones. Rather it is a search to match what your parents need with what is offered by a place where they might live. Your friends may recommend a facility for aged people in glowing terms. It was the perfect place for a neighbor's grandmother. But it may be a disaster for your mother. Or you may have heard bad reports about a certain home for the elderly and decided not to even bother checking it out— only to discover later that it offered exactly what your father needed.

Consider some of the following items.

How much privacy will your parents need? If this is to be a place for both of your parents, do you automatically assume that they will want to share a room? One of the big advantages of a board and care home for an elderly couple is that it will offer them more opportunities to still be together as a husband and wife in the way that they want. Not all elderly people like to sleep in the same room though. Find out what your parents think about each other's snoring, reading in the middle of the night, the time they get up, and the time they go to bed. This list is just to get the idea started. Let them finish it. They may have a big need to be together in the same house, but not the same room. Or they may have a big need to be in the same room and in the same bed. Your parents need to make those decisions. For your sake, I hope they agree. If they don't agree, the move to a another home may be an opportunity to deal with a problem that has always existed. Try to find a situation that does not make one win and one lose. It is important that both of them be pleased with the new place where they will live. If they don't agree on every detail, each will need to have something that is agreeable; so they both should feel they got something good out of the move.

If you have only one parent to be in a home, will she or he need a private room? Don't assume that one room one person is always the best arrangement. Sometimes room-mates provide security and social contact for one another. In good situations they help care for one another. In bad situations, they drive each other batty—and for some people that is not a long trip.

What parts of the home beyond their own room will be available to your parents? Is the dining room for mealtime only? Or is it also open for coffee breaks and snacks? Is there a place for the residents to be together to visit, play cards, share other activities? Will your parents want (and can they have) a TV in their own room so they can watch what they want? Is there a big-screen TV for all of the people to watch special events together? Is there a VCR connected with a communal TV, or would you need to provide that if your parents want it? Is cable TV available?

What secure places are available outside the house? Is there a porch, back yard, or other places with chairs for people to use so they can get fresh air and socialize with one another?

When you and others visit your parents where will they receive you? Must you always remain in their room with them to have privacy? Is the room large enough to have family groups come for a visit? Is there another part of the home that you could reserve for a birthday party? Is there a place in the house or yard where you could bring a picnic and share it with your parents but not everyone else?

6 • Level Two: Board and Care Homes

I went to visit Alfred a few days after he had moved from his own home to a board and care home. I thought he would be upset about the change. When I went into his new room I recognized all the furniture, including pictures and artificial flowers from his former home. However, the room was small and there was no chair for visitors. I was used to that and have often sat in a wheelchair or a portable potty chair as I visited friends in such homes. But before Alfred and I had finished our greetings the manager appeared with a chair for me. I immediately knew that my friend was staying in a home where he would receive good care. And he has.

The next issue is food. It is assumed that in bed and care homes the management provides all of the meals. Every family has its own idea of what good eating is. The supposed advantage of a board and care home is that it is home cooking; while a nursing home would offer institutional food. That may not always be true about either of these categories of care.

Find out what kind of food is served—and how it is served? Do all the people eat together in a dining room? Is it a happy place? Are the people given plenty of time to eat? Can meals be served in the residents' rooms when necessary? If so who makes the decision about when it is necessary? Would it be good for your parent to eat alone occasionally—or even all the time? Or is going to a dining room an important social and physical event?

Mom had lost interest in her personal appearance and hygiene. However the board and care home we chose for her had a nice dining room. The table was set properly with a pretty cloth and flowers—sometimes artificial but occasionally fresh. Mom responded to the occasion. She

119

felt a need to get dressed up for dinner.

Does the menu consider each resident's special dietary needs? Is enough food provided? too much? What will the people in charge do if your parents refuse to eat?

Are residents required to "dress" for dinner? Do the demands of management and the example of other residents make it necessary for your parents to keep themselves well groomed for meals—and other times? Visit the home at mealtime. How would you describe the way the people eat?

a) A family together for meal time.

b) A family being served together at a restaurant.

c) Individuals being served at a restaurant.

d) Strangers eating together at the same table.

Maybe the most important question: When you are visiting at mealtime, would you like to be invited to stay and eat with the others?

How much help do your parents need (and how much help is offered) in eating? Every board and care home must have certain rules that determine who is able to live there. Most of these rules are often symbolic signs of a person's ability for self-care. One of those rules may be that each resident must be able to come to the dining room for meals. Can your parents do it? Is there any reason to think that they will remain able to make the trip from their room to the dining room? They may also be required to cut meat, pour coffee, even take their plates and flatware from the table to the kitchen. Can they do it?

For most people eating is a social experience. Food is necessary not only for the energy received but also as a way of allocating time to be with people. People need to look forward to mealtimes. They need to enjoy the food, the way it is served, the people with whom they eat, and the people who serve it. Flowers on the table, proper place settings, cleanliness, and good smells are important.

6 • Level Two: Board and Care Homes

Some people also need to be a host or hostess. Do your parents? Could they invite you or someone else to stay for lunch with them? What would the cost be? How much advance notice would need to be given? Can they offer a visitor a cup of coffee? Is there a charge?

Another issue is medical needs. Although we are talking about a board and care home, not a nursing home, some health care may be provided.

Those who live in a board and care home have the same rights for home health care as if they lived in their own homes. County and other local governments may offer visiting nurse care. Other home care may be available to an individual through insurance and health care programs. The question is: Who is responsible to see that your parents receive the health care available to them from outside sources? Do not assume that the management of the board and care home will do the necessary paperwork. On the other hand, the people who run the home may have cut through the red tape to find services you would not have found on your own. Discuss this with the person in charge of the home before you make your decision.

In most cases elderly people need some medication daily. Will those at the home take the responsibility of seeing that it's taken? The home may require that all residents must be able to manage their own pills. If the management will not take the responsibility, and you feel your parents can't do it themselves, is it acceptable for you or someone else to take over that job?

Do your parents need regular exercise? Can they motivate themselves to take a walk or do other exercise? Are physical activities provided by the home? Are resources available, such as an exercise bike, horseshoes, or even a place to walk?

Next is laundry. Who will do your parents personal laundry? Some homes will provide laundry service for an extra fee; others include it in their monthly charge. A few have washers and driers available and expect the residents to be able to care for their own clothes. (That's a symbol of their ability to remain in that home; in other homes you would be expected to do the laundry for your parents, or to have it sent out at your or your parents' expense.) If one of your parents needs a shirt or dress pressed, who does it? If they need minor sewing repairs, who does it?

On related issues: How often are the beds changed and clean towels provided? Is there a rule stipulating so many times a week? Are there exceptions for accidents? Will your parents have a special problem with soiled sheets?

Now the hodge-podge of questions. Does the home provide any transportation—such as to the doctor, dentist, shopping, church, library? Is there an extra charge?

Who will take care of haircuts and other grooming needs? Will you have to take your parents to a shop? Will someone come in to take care of hair for a fee? What is the fee?

Could your parents have their own potted plants in their room? Some homes even allow residents to have a part of the garden, or at least an opportunity to have one tomato plant or rose bush outside. Would that be important to your parents? Are they allowed to have their own pets? Does the home have pets? If so, are they the kind your parents enjoy: fish, birds, cats, dogs? Would your parents be allowed to help provide for the pets owned by the management?

The board and care home where Alma lives has a special attraction. The managers keep exotic pigeons in the back yard. The pigeons are allowed to fly freely but they don't leave the beautiful back yard. Every afternoon the five residents in the home are invited to sit on the back patio for tea and cookies and to watch the pigeons have a snack at the same time. It is the social event of the day for that home.

What social services are provide by the home? Does any individual or group come to the home for religious services? Would your parents appreciate the kind of religious activities offered? Would they resent it?

Does the home invite people to come to show pictures, do craft work, tell stories, play music, or lead other such activities?

Does the home take its residents on field trips to a shopping mall, a picnic at a park, a movie or ball game? Are they required to go? Is there an extra charge?

Does the home provide books (their own or from a library)? Are they for the visually impaired? Does the home provide VCRs, CDs, tapes and records, puzzles, etc.?

This section has asked a lot of questions. The purpose is to help you evaluate your parents' needs. Not all of these questions will be important to you. (Please don't take this chapter and read it to the manager of a board and care home.) Write out the questions that apply to your needs— and add those issues important to you that I have missed. When people come to my office to plan weddings or discuss meetings and programs, I appreciate those who have a list. They have prepared to make the best use of my time and theirs.

Those who manage board and care homes are busy people. Recently I visited a member of my congregation in a board and care home. While there, I stopped by to see the owner to discuss this book. She had a box of plumbing tools in one hand and a shopping list in the other; I made an appointment to see her later.

Establish a good personal and professional relationship with those in charge. It may be okay to find out if drop-by visits are welcome so you can see how the places operates when visitors aren't expected. But when you want to use someone's time, make an appointment.

A Word About Expenses

The cost of the room in a board and care home is determined by what services you get. A private room costs more than one that has roommates. If the patient requires more attention, such as transportation, assistance with bathing and dressing, personal laundry, the cost will be more. Some facilities have one rate and give everyone the same service. Others have a basic price but may add to the cost if extra services are requested. Be aware of the possibilities before you make a decision.

Look at the Building

I've saved the part that you see first to be considered last. Because the building is the most visible part of the care your parents will receive, it often attracts the most attention. Someone will ask where your parents live. When you tell them, they may say, "Oh, I've seen that place." They will judge the facility where your parents live by what they have seen when they drove by the house. But you must make your decision primarily about the people and services that are provided in that house. A beautiful yard and attractive house—while reflecting the facility's values and priorities—do not guarantee a loving and caring place to live. A humble-appearing home may be filled with warm and concerned people.

First, look at the neighborhood. How near is it to you and to others who will visit your parents in their new home? You will be making that trip often; it is to your advantage to have your parents nearby. It is also to their advantage because you can drop by more often—and they will have more opportunities to be invited to your home. However, there may be good reasons why they need to be a distance from your home. The most obvious may be that no facility is near you. They may need to be close to medical care facilities. They may need to have specialized care that is best offered in another neighborhood.

Look at the community where they will live. Will it seem like home to your parents? Is it their kind of place? One of the advantages of a board and care home is that it is most often a part of a residential area. Perhaps the house is on a street that children use to walk to and from school every day. To many old people the joy of seeing those children would be much more important than watching TV. This may sound like a small thing, but beyond the privilege of being a little bit involved in the lives of children, the old people would also have a sense of time passing during the day. It would also give them an awareness of weekends, holidays, and vacations, helping them to stay oriented in life.

A board and care home often also provides neighbors. The residents of the home have a feeling of being in a community. There are people to speak to as they walk by. They can "protect" their neighbors by keeping an eye on the houses while the owners are away at work during the day and on trips on weekends. They can know who got a new car, see which house is for sale and wonder what the asking price is. Again, these are small things as we discuss them here, but they are part of a pattern that is good for elderly people to have.

We live next door to a board and care home. We get to know most of the people who live there—at least those who take walks or sit out on the front porch. Some of them invite us to see their rooms. Others have walked over to our house. One morning I found a little old man in my husband's garden. He was busy pulling weeds. I knew that he often forgot who and where he was. As I talked to him I realized that he thought it was his garden. At least he still knew the difference between weeds and vegetables! Maybe some people would think of the old people as a problem; we think they add to the value of our neighborhood.

The neighborhood may offer other advantages. If there is a park nearby, some of those who live in the home may enjoy a spring day sitting in the park. A sandwich, cookie, and soft drink would make the event into a picnic and could be a high point of the month.

If your parents are in shape to take walks on their own, check out the neighborhood for places that they might go. If they could not go by themselves, think of the times you will visit them. Sitting in a room with an elderly parent for even half an hour can become tedious. Think of how you might plan walks with your parents when you visit them. Also find out if other people who visit them could take them for a walk. In some cases a member of the staff might do it, but don't expect it.

Consider the sidewalks in the neighborhood. Do the curbs have ramps that make it possible for wheelchairs to be navigated across the streets? Are there steep hills that would be impossible for wheelchairs and difficult for some people to walk up or down? Is the area well lit at night?

Now look at the house itself. All the safety factors listed in the previous chapter apply to a board and care home also. In addition, there are other considerations that apply especially to this category of care.

Many board and care homes have been private homes remodeled for this business use. In order to provide more private rooms other bedrooms have often been subdivided and rooms that were not for sleeping have been converted into bedrooms. This may present some problems to watch for.

First, does the room have a closet that will serve your parents' needs? Is it a built-in closet or a piece of furniture? Is the room large enough that you could bring in a wardrobe if necessary?

Next, is the bathroom easily accessible to the room? Remember that many old people get up several times during the night to use the bathroom. Will that trip be difficult or dangerous for them? Has the management solved the problem by having portable toilets in the room? That may help, but those are not pleasant pieces of furniture to have around—especially when one has guests.

How difficult would it be to remove your parents from the room in case of fire? Would the only way out be down one hall? How many other people, possibly in wheelchairs, would be using that hall? Is there a window (assuming the room is on the first floor) that would allow your parents to be rescued? If the room is on a second floor served by an elevator, what are the other options of getting out of the building in case of fire?

One of the major things you will notice about the house is the smell. Perhaps the smell of urine causes the greatest hostility against homes for aged people. In the forty-some years that I have been visiting nursing homes, there has been a great improvement in this area. Increased health codes, competition, and new disinfectants have improved the smell in homes. Don't judge a home by one whiff—it could be that you arrived immediately after a problem developed. But do watch to see how the problem is handled. Old people should not be scolded or isolated because they cannot control their bladders or bowels.

Also pay attention to good smells—especially if you think they are there to cover offensive odors. A home for elderly people should not smell like a teenager trying to cover the smell of alcohol on his breath. But good aromas can be included for the right reasons. Fresh flowers are beautiful to the senses of sight, smell, and touch. Room fresheners, especially in the bathroom, are a good idea. Notice if the kitchen is close enough to the living areas so the residents can anticipate their meals as they smell what's cooking.

Is the home cheerful? Is there enough light? Is it properly heated in the winter, and cooled in the summer?

Can your parents have their own phone in their room? Will there be a cost of installation as well as the monthly bill? If they do not have a room phone, can they receive messages via another phone? Can they use the phone when they want to?

How will their mail be delivered to them? Do they have a secure place in their room to keep private and valuable items?

Finally, is this house a home for your parents?

How Will Care Giving Be Shared?

One of the chief advantages of a board and care home for your parents is that you will have a greater opportunity to be more involved in caring for them. By searching for the right home, and by negotiating with the management, you may remain more involved in the daily lives of your parents than if they lived in a retirement or nursing home. There are two good reasons for you to consider such an arrangement. First, both you and your parents may want you (and others in the family) to be responsible for normal family activities, even if they do live in a different home. Second, you may reduce the cost of the board and care home by providing as much service as you can.

When you are checking the board and care homes in your area ask if your parents can bring their own furniture with them. I doubt that you would find an unfurnished room any less expensive than a furnished one, but there may be an emotional advantage. One of the most difficult parts for most elderly people as they consider leaving their own home is the idea of giving up their own furniture. It may help if some of their things will be used in the homes of their children; they can hope to still see their treasures again. But it is even more helpful if they can take some furniture with them. Their belongings remind them of previous homes and precious memories.

Also check to see if a prospective home allows its residents to hang pictures and knickknacks on the wall. Is there room for them to bring their own TV and record players? Can they bring books, house plants, magazine holders, and other personal items? For some people these items are very important. Their transition to a different home would be easier if they could take something with them to make them feel at home. Not everyone can have as positive an attitude about giving up their personal property as the following woman:

> There's one advantage of having Alzheimer's. This is the time of life that we have to give up all those things that we have collected since childhood. With my disease I forget that I had them anyway.

At many board and care homes you can reduce the monthly charge by doing the laundry and providing transportation for your parents. If those services are not provided anyway, your monthly rate will be less. If they are included in the monthly charge, you may be able to reduce the expense by providing the care yourself. Plus, you will have something to do when you visit your parents. Visiting your parents in another home is going to be very different than having them in your home or seeing them in their own home. A project such as laundry, or a trip to the library, doctor or dentist may be welcomed by both of you. In a few cases you may be able to include room cleaning—at least making the bed—as a project that you and your parents share together.

If you are going to visit your parents at a set time each day, you may consider providing one meal for them. Some people visit their family in a home either on the way to work or on the way home. One could be at breakfast time, the other dinner. Or perhaps you could take lunch to your parents. In some cases different members of the family could take turns providing a meal for a person in a board and care home. Such arrangements would depend on the experiences of the management and the availability of the family. Of course, it would require dependability from the family. The management of the home would need advance notice of any changes—as would your parents.

As you visit the home you may meet the families of the other residents. Are there ways that you can work with them to provide care for their parents at the same time you care for your own? If you are going to take your mother to a movie, you might take someone else's parent too. The residents of the home might enjoy sharing activities with one another, and it might help them do more things together in the home. In return, the families of other residents can include your parents in their activities.

Regulations for Board and Care Homes

In recent years many communities have established safety and others codes for board and care homes. These codes are established for homes who have a certain number of residents (not related to the owner) living in the homes. Most homes for only a few outside of the family residents are not under any community supervision.

In many places the management will post the rules required by their local governments. Look for fire inspection certificates and notices that the kitchen has had a current inspection, if those are required in your area.

Appendix 2 is a voluntary patients' rights form used by an association of board and care homes in my community. This is not required by law but is an example of the advantages of a home belonging to a local association that requires certain standards. Ask the management of the homes you visit what legal and voluntary codes they adhere to.

Government rules and association regulations do not guarantee perfect service for your parents in any home. But they give you a basis to evaluate the minimum precautions that will be enforced. You will probably want to look for a place that offers more than the legal necessities.

Is This a Temporary Place?

By definition a board and care home may be only a temporary answer for your family. Your parents can stay in such a facility only as long as they do not need full-time nursing care. Many people spend their last years in a board and care home. Others stay for a number of years and then move to a nursing home.

You might think that it would be easier to find a place for your parents that has a variety of levels of care. That way they could get settled in the place now and, when the time comes for more care, they would just move from one section of the facility to another. In some cases that idea is correct (and it will be considered in more detail in the next two chapters).

However, there are advantages of being in a board and care home, even if one must move to a nursing home later. First, often the board and care home is less expensive. Because it offers less care, it can charge less for its services.

Second, a board and care home is less institutional in appearance and in operation than an assisted-living or nursing home. It may be easier for your parents to make the initial adjustment from their own home to a board and care home.

Few decisions in life are permanent. You must decide what is best for your parents under the present circumstances and for the future—as far as you can see.

—— 7 ——
Third Level:
Assisted Living

The term *assisted living* accurately describes all levels of people helping people. I can't think of a time in my life when I didn't need some assistance from others. Learning to accept and give assistance from one another is an important part of social adjustment.

In the context of providing homes for elderly people, *assisted living* has a special meaning. It is a good term to describe the level of need between that of one's own home or a board and care home and the services provided by a nursing home. Though there may be wide overlaps on either side of the scale, there is a need for assistance for people who can provide for many of their own needs but who need help in defined areas. For the purposes of this book, the large numbers of retirement homes and villages that are springing up everywhere will be regarded as assisted-living facilities. While not all assisted-living facilities are retirement communities, all retirement communities offer assisted-living programs of some kind.

Assisted-living facilities are the most visible, and appear to be the most delightful, of all services offering housing for elderly people. Most of them are for-profit businesses, though some are operated by churches and other public organizations. And most of them can afford to advertise. I am writing this chapter during the winter months in Tucson, Arizona, where many "snow birds" come for the season. Our TV and newspapers are filled with ads for local retirement communities. They offer invitations to an open house, a free meal to look at their facilities, and other incentives to attract future residents. All this advertising can help you in your search for a place for your parents; just be aware that your community probably offers many more facilities than those with lots of public exposure. Use the advertising and the information it offers as one source of information that you will use in your decision, but don't let it be your only source. Above all, don't select the first place you check out—unless you follow up by looking at many other places and then return to the first.

Some retirement communities require their patrons to buy their apartment in the facility. In most cases the arrangement is like buying a condo or an apartment in a large building. There are two prices that the buyer must consider: the cost of the unit and the monthly or quarterly fee for maintenance. The unit becomes the personal property of the buyer and a part of his or her estate. Your family's decision about buying such a unit would depend on your financial situation and the stability of real estate in your area.

The purchase of a unit is far different from the entrance fee charged by some retirement communities and nursing homes. This fee, which is often required before your name can be put on a waiting list, is not a payment for property. It is payment for services. In most cases those services are continued until the buyer's death. Typically, if the one who pays the fee dies a short time later, none of the payment is returned to the estate. On the other hand, if the buyer lives a long time, no additional charge is made— though there will be other monthly expenses. Though this method was widely used at one time, it rarely exists today. Be sure to check out the financial stability of the institution before making such an investment

Just a Little Help, Please
The first step toward assisted living happens for many married couples after the children have left home and they decide their house is too big. As they look for something smaller, they evaluate some other needs. They may decide they want assistance in some or all of the following areas:

Lawn care
Repairs and painting
Security
Window washing, cleaning
Transportation
Food service
Shopping

For those and other reasons, many still-active and healthy people choose the freedom of living in mobile-home parks, apartment complexes, and private homes that include common property and an overseeing association.

When I grew up we never locked the doors of our house when we left—I don't think we even had a key. Then I went through those years of always checking the locks. Now I like the freedom we have in our complex. Someone else takes care of protecting the place. I'm at home again.

Some home-owner associations provide not only lawn care but also maintenance of the outside of the buildings. They also offer security features. All of this is provided for a monthly or quarterly fee. People who chose these services for themselves are getting used to the idea of assisted living. They are freed to do the things they want to do because someone else is helping them. Understanding the value of assistance may be helpful for older people who need to increase the amount of assistance they are willing to accept.

Apartment complexes, mobile-home parks, and home associations may also offer swimming pools, recreation centers, and laundry services. All of these things provide assistance for people who can take care of themselves but who like the idea of paying a little more to get some help. Those who have made such decisions for themselves will be able to live independently longer because they have already asked for some help. They have also learned that asking for help doesn't hurt at all. It's a sensible thing to do.

A Little More Help

It's an old joke to say that statistics show that those who have more birthdays live longer. However the extra years will eventually mean a need for extra care. A balance between a person's desire to care for self and the willingness to accept help from others is an important part of adjustment to age.

When you need to become a part of your parents' decisions, you may want to point out to them how they have already accepted help from others. Use real illustrations from their lives of times when they gladly asked for others' assistance. Also, you may want to remind them of how they have reached out to others. Those who have been willing to give help can now receive it.

Mother always helped other people. It was her career. When there was a death in a family, she was the first one there with a casserole and a homemade pie; she did the laundry for friends who were sick.

As she got older she complained when she couldn't help others. I reminded her of the joy she received by helping others all of her life. Then I told her that the way she could help others now was to let them help her—so they could enjoy helping her as she had enjoyed helping others. I don't know if she ever fully accepted my logic, but she tried.

Is it time for your parents to request, "Just a little more help, please"? If so, then help your parents find the place that offers the help they need.

Do Your Parents Need Physical Help?

Often elderly people can no longer live in their home because they are handicapped and must be in a wheelchair or a walker. Perhaps they are losing their sight and need a place designed for the visually handicapped. It is expected that assisted-living facilities will have all the things needed for physically handicapped people. That includes ramps for wheelchairs, halls with handrails, elevators for multi-floor facilities.

Assisted-living homes most often provide each couple or individual with their own apartment or room with a kitchenette. Can all the appliances be operated from a wheelchair? Is the microwave above the stove—or is the freezer at the top of the refrigerator—and out of reach? Is there enough available storage space within easy reach?

Check the bathroom. Do your parents have strong preferences about showers versus baths? Do they have a choice? Could both of them use the bathroom at the same time—especially if one or both are in wheelchairs?

Does the institution offer special units for those with sight problems? Check the appliances in the kitchen. Can you use all the controls with a sense of touch rather than sight? Is the lighting adequate? Is there an easy way to increase the amount of light available? If your parents are blind or near blind, close your eyes and walk around the living space. Are there barriers that would be difficult for them?

How easy is it to open and close windows and drapes? Are the light switches accessible and easily operated? Check the location and ease of use of heating and cooling controls. Are the doorknobs easily reached and turned?

Do Your Parents Need Security?

Another reason that many people want their parents to live in some kind of special place for the elderly is security. Often the elderly people give this need a lower rating. But they need to be aware that criminals look for easy prey—and they fall into that category.

Does the public have free access to the living units in the facility you are considering? In many assisted-living and retirement communities, one can drive up to an individual unit and ring the bell. For many elderly people this is a plus. They enjoy having visitors. Some even like to have door-to-door salespeople, evangelists, and poll takers ring their doorbell.

However, accessibility to visitors also means availability to the general public. Do you want someone to screen your parents' visitors? Do you feel that a salesperson, someone pushing religion, or others might take advantage of your parents? Do you worry that someone could use a scam to get into your parents' unit to rob and terrorize them?

Many facilites have a security system that requires visitors to call from a front gate or door and identify themselves. Then, the residents can unlock the door from their room. This offers some security. But, frankly, any visitor who pushes enough buttons will find someone to open the door and allow access to all the units. Other places have locked front gates. These two methods offer minimal, but helpful, security. They at least give warning that no resident is totally alone.

Other assisted-living homes require all visitors to enter through a front lobby. Some will ask for identification for anyone entering and will phone the resident for approval. Others depend on the fact that every visitor is seen and could be identified. Many places have video monitors that allow someone in a security office or reception desk to see all who approach the building.

Do the bathroom and bedroom have call buttons for emergency use? How far away is the person who is responsible to respond to the call? Is someone available to respond to a call twenty-four hours a day? Does the apartment or room in which your parents will live have smoke detectors? If their room is on an upper story, is there an escape route other than elevators in case of fire?

You will need to make a decision with or for your parents to find the balance between security that protects and security that stifles and isolates.

Do Your Parents Need Prepared Meals?

Many elderly people need some form of group living in order to have proper food service. Though this is seldom a primary reason for anyone, it is on the list for most people. The process of shopping, storing, preparing and serving food takes a lot of time and effort. Then there's the clean-up after each meal. Some aging people develop bad eating habits.

My grandfather was able to stay in his own home after grandmother died because two of my aunts lived on the same block. The deal was that he had to eat one meal a day at the home of one of his daughters. But grandpa was an independent man. He would stash a supply of the food that he liked and not show up for meals at my aunts' homes. After he missed two meals in a row one aunt checked and found that he had been living on canned oysters and crackers. So they changed the rules. His daughters took meals to his house and ate with him.

One of the advantages of assisted-living homes is that they often provide a good combination of home-cooked meals, plus meals provided by the institution. The price list might include a variety of possibilities. One may have all meals in the dining room. Or the residents may opt for eating one or two meals a day in the dining room and preparing the others in their own units. Each facility works out its own system, so ask questions.

Can your parents change the number of meals (and which meal it will be) from day to day, or week to week? If they miss a meal in the dining room, will they still be charged for it? Could your parents invite guests to the dining room and pay for extra meals? Would they need to make reservations?

Grandma always wanted me to stay for lunch when I visited her in her retirement complex. At first I thought this was an urge she still had from the days when she cooked big family dinners. Then I realized that I was her status symbol. It was a big deal for her to have a young person eat with her in a dining room filled with old people. I learned to enjoy her enjoyment.

Most assisted-living businesses recognize that mealtime is important for reasons beyond the food that is eaten. One of the main features in their brochures will be pictures of the dining room and examples of the menu. If you visit the facility, you may be invited to stay for a meal. Accept the invitation. Many times the food is served as though the dining room were operated as a semi-expensive restaurant. Tablecloths, flowers, and fancy table place settings are common. The dining room should be large enough to seat all the residents, so one group is not rushed through to free up tables for the next group.

Also give attention to those who serve the food. My experience in visiting such homes is that most places are aware that the people who serve the food are as important as the food itself. I have noticed young, neat, well-dressed waiters in the dining rooms of assisted-living homes. They appeared to be students working their way through school. The old people loved it.

Of course, the ideal picture I am painting here may not always be true. But the fact is that food service is an important, highly visible issue, and you are dealing with a business that needs good public relations. You certainly will be paying for good food service. Will you get your money's worth?

Also consider the meals that your parents may plan to prepare in their own kitchen. Who will do the shopping? Does the kitchen provide appliances and storage for full service or just for preparing snacks? Will your parents want to prepare meals in their own kitchen for family or other guests? Is that a good idea?

Do Your Parents Need Physical Activities?
Sometimes an elderly person or couple living alone will become physically inactive. One reason your parents may need assisted living is that they need to be encouraged to participate in exercise programs. As you look around, evaluate their needs and find out what is offered.

Some assisted-living homes have exercise rooms that include full gym equipment. Others have stationary bikes, walking trails, swimming pools, and other facilities to encourage individual and group exercise. One retirement home in my community is next door to a YMCA. They have arranged for all of their residents to have Y privileges at specified hours. Some have associations with golf courses. And, of course, there is shuffleboard.

Having opportunities for physical activity is one thing; taking advantage of those opportunities is another. Physical activity will greatly increase (and so will the monthly bill) if the home also has an athletic director who has specific aerobics, dancing, and exercise classes. Check the weekly activity calendar to see how many exercise programs are offered. Attend a few of the sessions to see how they are managed and if you think your parents would use the opportunities offered. You may be paying for something that they would not or could not use.

Do Your Parents Need Social Activities?

To some, social contact is even more important than physical exercise. It is easy for elderly people to withdraw from society and live in the past. If your parents have lived in one neighborhood for years, many of their friends and neighbors may have died or moved away. They may not make the effort to meet the new, and often younger, families that are moving into the neighborhood. A move to an assisted-living home may give your parents a new lease on their social life. You need to know what opportunities are available for social interaction.

Start by looking at the arrangement of the building itself. Is it designed for privacy? That is important for some people. But the price of privacy is that your parents will have less opportunity to casually meet others who live in the same facility. For example, two of the homes in my area have units that offer maximum privacy. When I visit them I forget that I am calling on someone in a large institution. Each home has its own mailbox at the front door, parking places, and direct access to the street. In other homes that I visit, the community mailboxes are a major communication area. People gather to wait for the mailman. Most don't expect to get anything but junk mail, but they enjoy visiting with their neighbors about the weather—and the new person who just moved into 144C.

As you look at the room or apartment where your parents might live, walk from that place to the other places where your parents would go—to the front desk, the parking lot, the dining room, other activities. Would they meet other people on the way? Are there places to sit down for a visit? Would they walk by other rooms or apartments where they could knock on a door for a visit? Would many others walk by their door?

If the facility you are considering is large—let's say over fifty units—are there natural subdivisions? Is there a cluster of living quarters that have their own mailboxes, day room, dining area? Would your parents have the opportunity of a smaller, more intimate community as well as a larger one to find more people who share common interests?

What special social activities are scheduled each week and each month? Are these events supervised by paid staff or volunteers? Do they offer the variety that your parents need?

Are religious services held in the facility? Is it a type of service or Bible study that your parents would want? If the institution is operated by a religious denomination, what special programs do they offer? If your parents belong to a different denomination, would they feel comfortable with any special requirements? Consider especially rules about diet, alcohol, and perhaps even dress code and music. Does the home have an official chaplain? Would your church be allowed to start or participate in worship services, Bible studies, choirs and other activities connected with church life? Are there restrictions regarding the celebration of any religious holidays?

What cultural events are offered by the home? Does the management plan field trips to movies, plays, concerts,

sports events? Is there an extra charge? If not, are you paying for something that your parents will not use? Are there
special events in the home? Do schoolchildren ever visit to
sing or perform in plays? Are there dances, monthly or
weekly birthday parties? Are the social events for all of the
residents? May they invite family and friends to join them?
Can a room be reserved for a private party that would
include some other residents plus outside guests? Is there an
extra charge? Can you bring in refreshments or order them
from the kitchen?

Does the management offer organized classes? If so would
they be the kind your parents would attend? Is there a craft
room? If so, are all materials provided? Is there an instructor
or is everyone on their own? Do the residents pay for the
materials they use? Some older people get upset at the idea
of participating in anything that might give the suggestion
that they are back in kindergarten. However, doing craft
work provides both social and physical experience. For
many people it also gives a sense of accomplishment—and
gifts to give to others. Some facilities have craft fairs that
become big social and financial events.

Your parents may surprise you. Some people who have
been social creatures all their lives become more reserved
and content to be alone when they grow older. You must
respect a sincere need to be alone, without making them
feel rejected or unneeded. It takes love and understanding
to know the difference. Other elderly people will find new
interests. You may be shocked to learn that your father likes
to weave baskets or that your mother wants to play bingo.
The fact that they have never done it before has nothing to
do with what they are doing now. A new interest in life may
help them make the adjustment to their new home.

All of this is to prepare you for a confusing reality. You
may select a place for your parents because it offers the
things that they have always enjoyed—but they don't like it.

Or you may find that your parents will participate in and enjoy things they never tried before.

Do Your Parents Need Health Care?

The next chapter will be about nursing homes that provide health care. However, many retirement homes do provide a minimum amount of care. In those institutions that have both assisted-living and nursing-care sections, the line between the two may be somewhat blurred.

You should not expect a retirement complex to have nursing service. However, you do need to know what plans are made for medical emergencies. Is there any arrangement with a hospital, doctor, or clinic? How does that arrangement fit in your parents' insurance program?

Will the management provide any kind of wake-up call to check on each patient? In some assisted-living communities, all residents must flip a card on the outside of their door each morning by a certain time. A staff member patrols the halls at an announced time each morning. If the card is not flipped, the staff person will knock on the door. If no one responds, he will use a pass key to enter the apartment and check on its residents. Is that kind of service important to you?

If your parents should decide to live in a retirement complex that also includes nursing facilities, it means that round-the-clock nursing service is available nearby. Would the medical personnel that are on duty in the nursing-care section be available for residents in the retirement section in an emergency?

What Do Your Parents Need to Feel at Home?

My wife and I moved to a new home after our three children were adults and out of the nest. Within a few months each of them had brought something to our home to leave with us (to display, not to store!). They too needed to know that this house was their home. We all have that feeling.

Your parents will also need more than an apartment or a room. They need a home. You will also need to know what it is that makes a place a home for them.

The most obvious answer is furniture. In some facilities the residents are expected to bring their own furniture—nothing is provided. In others, all of the furniture is in place; there's no room to bring your own. You may find a variety of options between these two extremes. Your parents may feel better if they can take their own furniture with them. It may not fit the decorating scheme of their new home and it may not be the proper type or size, but those are not the issues for people who want to make their own nest.

Will your parents be able to choose the color of paint for their place? the drapes? the floor covering? Can they add their own rugs or carpet? Can they replace towel racks? Can they add shelves? Can they hang pictures? Know the rules before you make the final decision.

Are pets allowed? Any restrictions on number and kinds? Could your parents have house plants or a window box? A few retirement apartments even allow the residents to have a little part of the yard as a place to plant flowers. If your parents have green thumbs, or if they grew up on a farm, such an opportunity may be more important than many more expensive services.

My mother-in-law and her eldest daughter share an apartment in a retirement complex. The daughter was slightly under-age when they moved in but was accepted because she was family. They are allowed to have a small garden plot in the back yard. They enjoy the exercise and the place to visit with others who also have gardens. And they grow some good vegetables for themselves and to use as gifts.

7 • Third Level: Assisted Living

Are there special rules about the number, the age, and the length of time for visitors? Can visitors, especially young children, use the swimming pool and recreation room? Some assisted-care homes have guest apartments that may be reserved (at a charge) for overnight company. Check out the cost.

Will your parents have any extra storage space for out of season clothes, Christmas decorations, other items that they cannot yet give up but will not fit in their living quarters? Can you rent a separate storage space?

If your parents have a car, is there a reserved parking space? Would a garage be available? Is that an extra charge?

Many of the above items may apply to your parents. Some may not. Most important of all is the fact that people make a house into a home. Speak of the new place as a home for your parents. If possible have a house-warming party with family and friends. Let your parents show off the new home and have the role as host and hostess. Give them a memory in their new home that makes it seem like a new chapter in life, but still a part of the same book.

What Will It Cost?

The category of assisted-living and retirement homes will offer you the widest range of costs in places where your parents might live.

You need to have an understanding of how much you can spend per month for your parents. It is not enough to know the dollar figure from each of the many places that you might consider. You will need to know what services are included in that figure. Some start with a small amount but when all the extras are added it may be more expensive than others that include the same services in their regular price.

You also need to know how long the present prices will last and if there is any limit on the amount that can be added in any one year. You may want to ask for a financial statement of the organization. It could be a part of a large corporation that is in financial difficulty. Find out the track record for increases in the monthly rates.

Also do not assume that the most expensive place is the best place for your parents. I recently had the need to visit two of the most expensive retirement homes in our city—a place known for expensive retirement homes. Each has lavish buildings and feels like an expensive hotel. In one I was promptly received at the reception desk and sent to the place I requested. I found helpful staff people and was impressed by the way I saw them working with the residents. At the other I waited a long time before anyone came to the desk. The person I was referred to was not helpful and treated my request to see a resident as an imposition on her time. Needless to say, I would recommend the first place over the second.

However, I tell the above story to illustrate a more important point. People are more important than buildings. Though I obviously would rather have my mother cared for in the first home, I would not make my decision on one visit; the rude staff person at the second home may have had a bad day. (As I got in the car I told myself that she might have been a very caring person who had just been at a patient's death.) Take the time to check out more than first impressions and the attitude of one staff person.

Also, the most luxurious place may not always be best for an elderly patient. The following story is from my own experience. Laura was a member of my congregation when I arrived and lived in the most expensive section of a facility that offered a range from independent living to nursing-home care. She had a large private home and her own private nurse. When I first called on her, the nurse said that Laura rarely spoke. I would have a communion service for her with little response from her.

7 • Third Level: Assisted Living

Through her nurses I learned that Laura's expenses were paid by her son who was very wealthy. However, the son died without mentioning his mother in the will. Laura did not get along with her daughter- in-law, who subsequently cut off her monthly allowance. Laura went from her private room and nurse to a shared room and regular care provided by the county. Her life improved markedly. She attended the worship services we held in a day room. She talked to people and participated in other events. She was a lot happier person in her poverty than she had been in her wealth.

But poverty doesn't guarantee contentment either. Try to plan your parents' finances so they can continue to live at the level to which they have become accustomed. Many elderly people say they could plan for themselves if they knew the exact date they would die. You could do the same for your parents if you had that information, but you don't. The ideal situation is to be able to pay for their monthly expenses from their Social Security check, any other retirement program, and the return from other investments that they might have. When you need to use some of their principal, you will lower the amount of return in interest or dividends.

As you look at your parents' present income you also need to know if it will or will not change in the future. Many retirement funds provide a stated amount that will not go up for inflation. What seems like a good monthly income now might be inadequate five years from now. If their income is based on interest on investments, the interest rates could go down. If you need the advice of financial planners, look for it.

How Long Will It Last?
The institutions that offer assisted living for elderly people provide a step. For many people it is a long step. If their needs stay in the range provided by the facility they have chosen, they may live there for years—even the rest of their lives. For others a sudden change in health can increase

149

their needs, and they will require either a place that offers more assistance or the full services of a nursing home. You cannot plan for every possibility. But you can be aware of what your parents' present needs are and what additional services are available to them in case their needs increase.

8

Level Four:
Nursing-Care Homes

Just as many people call all soft drinks "Cokes" and all facial tissues "Kleenex," many would refer to all of the facilities discussed in the previous two chapters as nursing homes. In fact, the Yellow Pages of your local phone directory may list them all under the category "Nursing Homes." The term has become a generic phrase to include any place where elderly people live. However the purpose of this book is to help you to see the individual trees in the forest—the individual facilities among the large number that care for elderly people—so we are using more restricted definitions.

Nursing homes are those that offer professional nursing care. They also provide all of the other special cares discussed in previous chapters such as a room, meals, security, physical activities, and social contacts.

The big question for your family may have been, "Do Mom and Dad need to live in a nursing home?" If everyone has agreed that the answer is yes, you may feel that you are over the hump. You have made the big decision. But climbing mountains and making decisions have a lot in common—when you get to the top there is always another mountain or another decision. In this case, the next question is, "Which nursing home will be best for Mom and Dad?" The answer is to find the best match between what your community offers and what your parents need.

You may already know about many of the nursing homes in your community because you have driven by them, and perhaps even visited friends in some of them. However, these home are going to take on a different appearance when you are considering them as a possible home for your parents. What was casual before becomes critical now.

Become aware of the variety of nursing homes in your community. Many may be on side streets or in a part of town you don't normally see. Look through the telephone books and ask your local Council on the Aging to find out what is available. You may not need to visit each home, but you want to make sure that you are checking out those that offer the best care for your parents.

Who Owns the Home?

You should know who owns the homes that you are considering. Even though the staff that is on duty in the rooms, kitchens, and social areas of the home are far more important than the person in the front office, there are several reasons why you need to know who owns the place.

First, is there an obvious possibility that the nursing home will go out of business within the next several years? Any business, public or private, may have financial difficulties. If the home you are considering is a part of a large corporation, you need to know if the corporation itself is financially sound and if the home in which your parents will live is profitable for the company. If the individual home is not showing a profit, it could be closed. Or it could change management, which might include a change in both personnel and policy.

> My mother had been in a nursing home for over two years, and both she and I were very pleased with the care she received. Then the home was sold. We were never told about the change, but suddenly many of the staff that we appreciated the most were gone. We found that some had been fired and others had left. The ratio of patients to nurses went way up. Then I read in the paper that the food services had failed to pass the state inspection. We went from a very satisfactory to a very unsatisfactory situation in a short time.

Next, the ownership of the facility explains the reason for its existence. Neither nursing homes nor any other business come into existence like wildflowers. They are planted—and they are planted for a reason.

Some nursing homes are private businesses. In come cases it may be a small business operated by an individual or a family who have only one nursing home. In other cases a home may be operated through the sale of stocks or bonds. There are large chains of nursing homes operated by corporations. In all of these cases, people have invested their own money to make more money; it is a legitimate business venture. But if the business does not show a profit, it will have to close. You will need to know that the home is operated on good business principals. Unless the home fulfills the purpose of those who started it, it will not stay in business.

Other nursing homes are operated by city, county, or other local governments. These tax-supported nursing homes are the modern-day replacements for the old county poor farms. Such homes are for those who have limited or

no income. In some communities the local government contracts rooms for indigent people in privately owned homes.

If your parents have no savings and only a small income,
you will need to check what is available for them. A word
of assurance: In my experience (limited but, I think, typical)
I have found that tax-supported nursing homes offer services as good as many privately owned homes. Their buildings, staff, and services are comparable to all but the most
expensive private homes. The one difference is that they
cannot reject anyone who needs their services. Therefore,
they may have more difficult patients. Certain areas of the
home may not look or sound as peaceful and organized as
you would like for your parents. Residents are divided into
categories according to their needs. Private nursing homes
can refuse patients who are beyond their help; tax-supported homes will not. However, the publicly owned nursing
home also provides good care for many who are in the more
typical range of those who need nursing care. Other nursing
homes are owned by religious and fraternal groups. The fact
that they are owned and managed by a charitable organization does not mean that they are free—and in most cases
they still need to cover their own expenses, if not show a
profit.

As you explore the possibility of your parents living in
such a home, you need to know first if they would be accepted. In some cases these institutions can accept only those
who belong, or have family connections, with their organization. However, most will accept people who otherwise fit
their stated purpose of providing health care. Would your
parents want to live with the policies of the religious or fraternal group that makes the decisions? Would there be restrictions on diet, dress, or other activities that would not be
acceptable to your parents or your family? Find out the
requirements before your parents move in. Do not make
demands or expect exceptions that violate management's

reason for operating the nursing home. Since you (or your family) will be paying for the services provided, it would be natural for you to have a customer mentality—that is, "Since I am paying for what I want, you need to provide what I need." However, nursing homes managed by charitable groups have a service mentality: "We are here to provide something for you—what you see is what you get."

You will also want to know what the relationship of the home is with the sponsoring church or fraternal group. If the building is owned by the church or lodge, if the staff is regarded as employees of the same, it will be much more controlled by the religious and fraternal policies of the owners. In many cases nursing homes with a denominational label have a more distant connection to the official church structure. They may be operated by a board whose members—or at least a majority of them—belong to the church. However, they may be a separate organization and have no financial ties to the name on the stationery.

None of these issues will be a big factor in your final decision. However it is important for you to be aware of the basic philosophy of those who make the policy decisions. Looking for a nursing home will be a little bit like dating. If a lot of conflicts arise as you get acquainted, don't propose.

Nursing homes are the most highly regulated industry in the United States, with even more government regulations than the nuclear energy industry. Appendix 3 provides a copy of the residents' rights for a nursing home. All residents (or the person responsible for them) must sign this document before being accepted by a nursing home. Most people sign this document without reading it. I think it would be worth your time to carefully go through the rights statement to understand what issues are covered. Remember that the document is for the legal protection of the nursing home as much as for the residents and their families. Also be aware that this document cannot guarantee that every nursing home will provide all of the rights that it promises. I would look for a nursing home that regards these rights as a minimum of the rights that they want to offer their residents—rather than one that sees this list as the maximum that they must offer.

Who Is the Nurse in the Nursing Home?

Suppose you and your family have decided that you can afford so much a month to provide a place for your parents. (I do not dare to include even an estimated amount because of the range of prices in various parts of the county—and because any figure I use as I write this may be unreal by the time you read it.) So you drive to look at three rooms that are available at the price you can pay. The first is in a board and care home, the second is in an assisted-living home, and the third is in a nursing home.

You will be shocked to see the difference in the three rooms. For the same price you can receive more privacy and a much more attractive place in the board and care and the assisted-living homes. The room in the nursing home will probably look very plain when compared to the others. I warn you about this ahead of time, so you do not rush into a premature decision. In the nursing home, the price is in the word "nurse." The monthly payment is going for trained, professional people not buildings.

The amount of nursing care provided will vary from place to place. As you visit a nursing home you will see lots of staff people dressed in white. To you they may all look like nurses, but the payroll people don't see them that way. Some are nurses' aides. Others are Licensed Practical Nurses. Some are orderlies. Others are therapists—physical, occupational, respiratory, and others. Some are Registered Nurses and some are medical doctors.

I work in a large nursing home and I am amazed that

most family members who visit our residents think that all women dressed in white are nurses, and that all men in white are doctors. Our doctor is a woman. Many of the nurses and orderlies are men. But we can't spend all our time explaining what we do, because we are busy doing it.

You need to be aware that different nursing homes provide different levels of medical care. Some have a doctor on staff, others have a doctor who serves as a medical director and is on call and who consults with other medical personnel on the staff. Therapists with special training may also be available in homes that offer selective care. You need to know what is offered in case you need it. On the other hand, your parents may not need some of the special care that you would be paying for in some homes.

Also check the nurse-to-resident ratio. In some places one nurse may be on duty in a place with many residents. Other places may provide one nurse for every four patients. You can easily see why the cost would be much higher in the second case. Keep in mind that a nursing home has three shifts of workers every day and that the nurse-to-resident ratio might be different on each shift. As you are collecting information, find out the nurse-to-resident ratio for each of the shifts. Medical personnel are not the only extra expense that nursing homes have. They also will offer hospital beds in some rooms, medical equipment and supplies, and medical insurance—all of which increase their operating cost.

Special Needs—Special Services
Some nursing homes offer special services for limited needs of certain patients. Others have different sections for different needs within the institution. Each special need may require medical personnel with advanced training in that area and may also require special equipment and activities. If your

parents need the care of a nursing home, they are already under the care of a physician. Their doctor will tell you what kind of special care they will need in a nursing home—and perhaps even give you a list of facilities that offer that care.

By knowing the kind of care your parents need and what service each of the nursing homes in your community offers, you can save time in your search. The list below could be the sections offered by a variety of institutions, or it could be a list of specialized nursing homes available to you and your family. Different areas will have different names for their categories of care; the following categories are typical rather than exact.

Transitional Care

Because of limitations imposed by insurance companies and Medicare on the number of days that a patient may remain in the hospital, many people must leave a hospital but are physically unable to return home. In some cases the patient still needs medical care. In others, the family is not able to provide the care needed. For this reason many nursing homes offer a unit (and some have opened solely for this purpose) of transitional care. They are halfway houses between hospitals and nursing homes.

In most cases, the decision regarding a transitional care unit is easy. The hospital has an agreement with such a home, or perhaps the nursing home is owned by the hospital or its parent company, and the transfer from one to the other is like moving from one section of the hospital to another.

Patients may stay in a transitional care unit for weeks and even months. During that time you will have an opportunity to find a place for them to live when they have recovered enough to be receive another type of care.

Our family was not ready to accept the fact that Dad could

8 • Level Four: Nursing-Care Homes

no longer live alone. When the doctor suggested the transitional nursing home, we were upset. Then the doctor explained the purpose of this halfway place. We accepted it as a place for Dad to be while he recovered. But it also proved to be a halfway experience for our family. We had time to accept the fact that recovery for Dad did not mean going back to be like he had been last year. We had to adjust to his new health situation and make decisions accordingly.

Just as the transitional care unit may be regarded as a gradual move out of a hospital, it can also be an entry point into a more conventional nursing home. The halfway care could be provided by a home that offers other levels of care, allowing your parents to remain in the same facility after they no longer need the transitional care. In that case, your choice of a place for the halfway care would have more long-range implications. In addition to investigating the kind of care offered in the transitional unit, you would want to look at what other facilities the same home offered, and determine whether they would match your parents needs.

Subacute Care
Subacute units or homes may offer many of the same services as the transitional care units and can serve the same purposes. However, some facilities will distinguish between the two because the subacute care offers more long-range care. While the transitional care unit is preparing for the patients to improve and require less medical supervision; the subacute care unit also includes those who are more seriously ill and may not recover. If your doctor recommends subacute care for your parents, you have fewer homes to consider for them.

For the record, not every patient who goes to a subacute nursing home dies there. Many elderly people still have strong will power and general good health in other areas of their bodies that help them recover from a specific and serious illness. If you must choose a facility for subacute care, plan for the next step if and when your parents' health improves.

Hospice Care

Hospice care is for those who are dying within a specified time. Since the use of a hospice is only for terminally ill patients, it does not come under the long-range decision making that is the subject of this book. The decision regarding using the services of a hospice would probably be a book in itself. However, I have included hospice in this list because hospitals and nursing homes often have hospice units. Your parents may not be terminal in the sense used by hospice workers. However, you may be aware that in a matter of months or a few years your parents will be in that category. If you are at least aware of the process now, you will be better equipped to seek possible hospice care later.

Behavioral Care

Some people have a negative image of nursing homes because they feel that the homes are there to serve only those who have serious behavioral problems. In reality a small percentage of people in nursing homes are in units that provide behavioral care.

Behavior problems are one of the most difficult medical needs for families to handle. People with other serious medical difficulties usually are able to stay in their own homes, board and care homes or assisted-living homes. But behavioral difficulties require professional care. Nursing homes can provide that care.

Some of the most common behavioral problems are uncontrollable anger, uncontrollable motions, talking or screaming, delusions and other forms of physical and mental behavior that disrupt normal living. Family members often think the patient is doing such things on purpose. Well-meaning relatives and care givers may try to bribe or threaten those with such problems into normal behavior. But such problems are not self-willed. They cannot be self-corrected.

> Mom calls for Benny, her dog, over and over again. He's been dead for nine years, yet she calls and calls. I don't think she even connects what she is saying with the dog. It's just a word that got caught in her mind and she says it over and over. There's no point in telling her to stop it. Certainly there is no point in getting her another dog.

Care in a nursing home can be very helpful to you and to members of your family who have such needs. First, you are getting proper care for your parents. Your parents will not be punished for their behavior; they will be encouraged and assisted in improving it. Even the most difficult patient can respond to love and attention.

> In my work in a nursing home I regularly walked past a woman who always jabbered. Most of the time her words and sounds made no sense. Even though she wasn't under my care I spoke to her each time I passed. I then realized that each time I passed she would say, "He doesn't even look human." While her comments may have deflated my ego, I told myself it was not a professional opinion and continued to speak to her. Over the months I realized she was saying something else when I passed. Her new comment was, "He's the nicest man I know"— over and over again. I accepted that as a professional opinion. It showed me how much the simple act of saying hello to a person could help.

Sometimes family members and friends who visit a nursing home or unit for patients with behavioral problems are offended by what they see. The doors are locked. Rarely is there a place for residents to go outside for fresh air and sunshine. Some patients are tied in a bed or wheelchair. Some are obviously sedated. That is not a pretty picture—unless one thinks of what the picture would be without the protection provided by the nursing home for its residents.

Doors must be locked. Some of the patients are unaware of where they are, and they could wander away. Others are compulsive walkers. A nurse recently told me that one of the patients I visit regularly often walks the halls twenty hours a day. Think what might happen to her if she got outside of her unit. While doors must be locked to protect the patients, it can be done in a way that respects their need for a normal atmosphere.

> I felt awful the first time I visited mother. I stood outside a large gate made of iron bars. I had to wait for the sound of a loud buzzer and a click that indicated I could open the door. I found my mother crying in her room. She asked me, "What have I done wrong? I should have had a trial. I can't remember what I did." Then I realized that she thought she was in jail. My heart broke. For that and other reasons we moved her to another home. The door is still locked—but it is a door not a gate. There are discreet pushbuttons on a security lock to open the door. Only staff members know the combination, but they are always available.

In the past a few nursing homes may have overused restraints, both physical bonds to secure patients and drugs to sedate them. Sometimes such methods were used for groups rather than for individual needs. It may happen in rare occasions today, but it is illegal. No person may be restrained without an order from a physician. The restraints must not be punitive and they must not exceed the amount of control required by the individual's condition. The restraints may be used only when they are needed to protect the patient from him- or herself, or to protect other patients from the behavior of one.

As you visit a nursing home you may see a sweet little lady tied in a chair. She may ask you to free her. Never do it. And never condemn the staff or institution without knowing the reasons for the restraints.

People who work in a behavioral care home or unit are under constant pressure. They need a special ability to not respond to abnormal behavior with inappropriate behavior of their own. Before you decide on a behavioral care unit for your parents, watch how the staff treat the residents. Watch not only the professional medical staff, but also those who serve food and those who clean the facilities. Do they respect the residents? Do they say hello? Do they speak to them before they touch or move them? Do they smile and make casual talk—even to residents who cannot take part in a conversation? Are they alert to conflicts among residents, and do they separate the combatants without scolding? Can they clean up after someone who has vomited or urinated, without making a federal case out of the issue?

Recognize that if you are considering placing your parents in a behavioral care unit or home, you have already been under extreme stress. Their need probably did not arise suddenly. Over a period of time you have seen them develop problems that make it impossible for you to keep them in your home or in another level of care. You may have been told that you must take your parents out of a board and care or an assisted-living facility. You may have felt the pressure of their increasing problem in your own home. In any case you probably denied the problem for a while. You told yourself that they were only having a bad day—or that you were having a bad day. You may have blamed the staff at another institution when the management told you that your parents were developing behavioral problems. But finally you have to face the fact that they need special care.

At first you might be willing to take the most controlled care available—the place for the most severely handicapped patients. Though that may be necessary, do not overreact. Get the opinion of your doctor and the supervisors of the nursing home.

> I've been a nurse on a behavioral care ward for ten years. If I could say one thing to all families who have relatives in this kind of care—or who are thinking about it—I'd say, "Don't feel guilty about letting us help take care of your family." People need help. It's as simple as that. Some families—especially sons and daughters—come in here to visit patients and show their guilt by making it difficult for the parents. They see the staff as competitors for their parents' attention, as though we are trying to replace them when we show love and care. I think they should be grateful that there are places like the one where I work—and for people like me who want to help them take care of their parents.

Realize that you can do your duty as a son or daughter better by working with the nurses and others in the home. You want your parents to have good care. The staff can provide better care if they see you as partners with them in providing for your parents.

Alzheimer's Units
In many nursing homes Alzheimer's patients are included in the section for behavioral care. However, as the public is becoming increasingly aware of Alzheimer's disease, many

nursing homes have separate sections for this need. For the purposes of this book those who have Alzheimer's fit in the category above. For your own personal needs you may want to read *Alzheimer's: Caring for Your Loved One, Caring for Yourself* by Sharon Fish (Lion Publishing).

Respiratory Care

Many people with respiratory problems need the special care of a nursing home. Even though they may be mentally alert and in otherwise good health, they may need special equipment in order to breathe. They also may need special therapy on a regular basis and medical people nearby at all times. Nursing homes that have a respiratory care unit provide those services.

Visiting a respiratory care unit shows a different view of a nursing home. To some it may seem more like a hospital because the equipment is more visible. However, the nursing home is providing maintenance care, with less emphasis on treatment in the sense of curing an ailment.

A respiratory care unit can provide a controlled environment. Furniture, drapes, carpets, etc. have been selected to reduce molds in the air. The heating and air-conditioning units may provide special filters. No flowers or flowering plants are allowed in the unit. Smoking is absolutely out of the question. The air is humidified or dehumidified according to local and seasonal needs.

Such units can provide a controlled environment that would be difficult to offer in your own home or in other types of care for elderly people. Your parents' physician and respiratory therapist will be able to recommend homes that have special units for this kind of care.

Specialized Isolation

Some nursing homes offer special units for those who must be isolated from the general population of the rest of the home. Most people are aware of AIDS today, but people infected with HIV are only one group among many who need this special care. Those who have TB, hepatitis, and other highly contagious diseases may need to be in an isolation unit.

An isolation unit is needed for two reasons. One, the patients may have illnesses that can be communicated to others. They must be in areas where staff, other patients, and visitors can easily be protected by necessary procedures such as disposable masks, gowns, and gloves. They may also have special security signs telling how all visitors must wash their hands.

However the isolation is also to protect the patients. Many times— especially in the care of AIDS patients— their health is so fragile that they dare not be exposed to the routine germs that we carry around with us every day. Some people need to be removed from the daily exposure to people that would happen in a private home or in other levels of care.

Your parents' doctor will tell you when and if you need this specialized care for them.

Rehabilitation Care

Rehabilitation care is another important section of many nursing homes. This service is for those who have had strokes, accidents, brain damage, or other medical problems that have limited their ability to move, walk, or speak. By definition a rehabilitation unit should be for temporary residents. After they are rehabilitated they should be able to return home. Sometimes that happens. In other cases the rehabilitation program is to prevent further deterioration of the patients' abilities or to improve their physical condition so they can be cared for in another section of the nursing home.

The need for physical therapy is one of the most obvious

reasons for a person to be in a nursing home. Families and board and care homes cannot provide the professional care needed. It would also be expensive in many cases to buy the necessary equipment. If your parents need rehabilitation therapy, the personnel and equipment in this section of the nursing home will be the most important factor for you to consider.

Respite Care

Many nursing homes have a respite care unit for day care only. The part-time residents many spend an agreed-upon number of days per week in the respite care center. This can become a long-term arrangement that allows the family to provide primary care while still giving the parents supervision during the workday. It is also a social diversion for the elderly people. Another advantage of respite care is that it offers an entry level for people who might object to living in a nursing home full time. Often elderly people enjoy the activities of a respite unit. They meet other people who also may become full-time residents of the home.

General Care

All of this may sound as though every nursing home, and every unit in such homes, is planned and staffed for specialized treatment. Not so. Many nursing homes serve the general population of elderly people who need some type of nursing care. The line between those elderly people who live in their own homes, board and care homes, or assisted-living homes and those who live in nursing homes is not determined by medical needs only. Some who have a high need for nursing care manage to get that care in other places than a nursing home. On the other hand, some who have low medical needs do not have family that can or will provide for them; they must live in a nursing home. The complicated rules of insurance coverage and public assistance sometimes also require that a person live in a nursing home in order to get financial help.

The general-care nursing home offers a place for people who have low medical needs. Nurses are available, but there is a higher patient-to-nurse ratio. Nurses may not be on duty twenty-four hours a day. Such a home can provide all the necessary nursing care for many people.

Which Will It Be?

As you look for a nursing home for your parents, your first task is to eliminate those places that do not fit your parents' needs. You may find a beautiful home with good staff and a low monthly cost, but if it does not offer the services that your parents require it must be marked off your list. New York City's Mayor Dinkins is credited with saying, "If you can buy an elephant for fifty cents it is a good deal—if you have fifty cents and if you need an elephant." A good deal in a nursing home is a good deal only if you can afford it and if it offers what you need.

After your first round of research you should come up with a list of nursing homes that offer what your parents need—and no more than they need. That list should include only those homes that are in your price range. Be aware that you cannot compare just the cost per month but must also include any extra charges, and what services will and will not be provided for that price.

You are fortunate if you still have a long list of appropriate nursing home for your parents. Though it may be a problem for you in terms of time and energy to check out a number of homes, look at it as a good problem. The more homes that offer the primary services that your parents need, the more opportunity you have to be selective about secondary needs.

8 • Level Four: Nursing-Care Homes

Start with Staff

The employees are the most important part of the home where your parents will live. Their professional qualifications and their personal attitude about the residents are of highest importance.

> I was visiting a friend in a nursing home when the fire alarm sounded. A nurse quickly told me it was a drill. I watched two staff members seal the fire doors and get all the residents into closed rooms. I was impressed with how they managed to work fast without alarming the patients. I thought, "What a nice place for old people to live." When the drill was over, I started to leave when I heard a supervisor in another unit scold an employee about something that had happened during the drill. The supervisor used a loud voice and abusive language, and the scolding was done in earshot of many residents. I thought, "What a terrible place for old people to have to live."

The above story illustrates the need to get more than one impression of the staff in a nursing home. Good, kind people can lose those virtues under stress. A rude or unkind staff person may be newly hired or soon to be fired.

Most people treat others as they are treated. If the management- level employees treat the rest of the staff with kindness and personal consideration, it will be easier for those who work with patients to treat them with kindness and personal consideration. People who work together in any place develop a group personality. Discover that personality.

Also be aware that the way you treat staff people will determine how they will respond to you. Anytime you interview someone in a nursing home about the possibility of your parents living there, and anytime you visit the residents' areas, the experience goes two ways. You are seeing how the staff operates—and they are seeing how you operate. If you show a suspicious or accusing nature, you are not establishing a good relationship with those who may be caring for your parents. Look for people who will work with you in providing care for your parents. Let them know you realize you need them and that you want them to enjoy your parents.

> I've worked in a nursing home more years than I want to admit and I have enjoyed the patients. They make my job worthwhile because I know I am helping them. My biggest problem is with their families and other visitors. They often upset the patients by their loud and inappropriate conversations. They are rude to me and others on staff by making unfair demands and by blaming us for things that we have nothing to do with. Some treat us like their personal servants. It's during visiting hours that I consider taking early retirement.

As you visit nursing homes, express your needs not your demands. Do not tell the staff how bad other nursing homes are, or repeat bad stories about other nursing home staffs. They have long ago learned that if you found faults with another place, you will also find fault with them. Look for good qualities in the staff and expect to find them. Most people live up to what is expected of them—and down to what they are suspected of.

Look at the Building
Nursing homes are regulated for safety and cleanliness. That does not mean every home lives up to the regulations. Some government agencies have regular inspections and enforce compliance to all safety rules. Others are more lax. You need not take over the job of safety inspector, but you do need to

know what happens in the day-by-day operation of the facility where your parents might live. Your job is to look more for compliance with the spirit, rather than the letter, of the law.

Are the public areas neat and clean? Do they smell good? Are the residents properly clothed and groomed within reason? What is your feeling about the atmosphere when you first walk into the building? Are you going to be embarrassed that your parents must live in such a place? Will you find yourself making excuses about the home when relatives show up to visit your parents? What will those excuses be? If you need to write to other family members to tell them about the home, what will you tell them that sounds good—and is true?

Uncle Al always enjoyed going to the church services held in the nursing home where he lived. The services were held in the cafeteria and lots of people attended. Then the management decided to remodel a room to be used as a chapel. They put in some stained-glass windows, an organ, and even a carpet. We thought the improvement was great. But Uncle Al was not allowed to go to church anymore because he could not control his bladder. The new carpet would have been ruined if Uncle Al urinated on it. So much for progress.

Now visit a room similar to the one your parents might live in. Could they accept it as home? Is it neat and clean? Is there enough living space? Is there enough closet and drawer space? Is there a place in the room that they could store private and valuable articles without fear of theft? Would you be allowed to do anything to make the room more personal for them? If the room must be shared, who picks the roommate? Does anyone monitor the relationship between roommates? If there is a personality conflict can one change rooms? Who decides?

How much time do the residents spend in their own rooms? Are meals ever brought to them? Under what circumstances? Could your parents have their own TV? Telephone? Pet? Some nursing homes do allow pets on the premises, but not the patient's own animal of choice. Instead they have a duty cat that visits rooms or stays in the day room. For many people a pet is good therapy. Others are allergic to certain animals. Some just don't like cats! Check it out.

Think about what you and others would do when you visit your parents. Would you stay in the room? Is there a garden area or a patio where you could visit? Would you have privacy?

What are the smoking rules and how are they enforced?

Drop by the home at mealtime. Would you enjoy the meal? Are individual diets considered? Are the residents given ample time to eat? Does anyone help them if they need it? Is mealtime also a social time for the residents and/or guests?

In all of these things remember that you are looking for a place for your parents—not for yourself. Be sure to think of their priorities for privacy, activities, diets, and the like. Also remember that their present needs may be far different than they were only a short time ago. Moving to a nursing home is a big event in the life of a person. It is important to maintain continuity with their previous experiences, but it is also a time when changes must be made—that's the point of the move. Help your parents understand (by understanding the issues yourself) what can be done to keep life as it was and what good changes must occur. If your parents won't buy the idea of "good changes" downgrade to "necessary changes."

The Location
You are looking for a place where your parents may live for

many years. This means you and others will be visiting them often. Where you go to make those visits is important.

Consider the people who will visit your parents. Who will visit most often? Whose needs are the most important? In order to get the care that your parents need you may have to drive by many other nursing home to find the one you need. However, the time spent driving either will take away from the time you spend with your parents or the time you spend with yourself, your family, your job. What about visitors who cannot drive? Is the nursing home near public transportation? Is parking available? Be aware of inconveniences before you make a decision.

Appreciate the Choices You Have

You are looking for the best place for your parents to live. You have accepted the fact that they need the care of a nursing home. Appreciate the fact that others are available to help you and your parents in your present situation. Make the most of the services they offer.

9

Living With Your Decision

Once you have made a decision, you need to live with it for a while before you put it into practice. Live with your decision by thinking how it will affect their lives—and yours. As you do this you are not necessarily opening the door to change your mind, though that might happen. But, more important, you are adjusting to a new event in your life, and you are thinking about ways to help your parents and others to also make the adjustment.

You may also have to make future decisions that will mean your parents must move again. You can prepare yourself for that possibility by allowing yourself to see that your present decision is made for present circumstances. New circumstances might mean a new decision later on.

Life Goes On

Depending on the amount of time you had to make the decision regarding your parents' place to live, you may have thought about little else in recent weeks. If you had a long time to evaluate the possibilities before it was necessary for your parents to make a move, you may also have had time to adjust your own life to the new situation with your parents. However, if your parents had a sudden change of health or other circumstances that required a sudden move, you may have put your life on hold while you helped your parents. You will need to re-establish your role with other members of your family, your job, and, most of all, yourself. Life needs to go on for both you and your parents.

You are not being selfish as you evaluate how much time you can give your parents. During a crisis all of us will forget the other members of the family and ourselves to help the one in need. But that works only during an emergency situation. Once a decision has been made and your parents have moved, you need to establish new routines of life for yourself. Your parents will also need to develop a new pattern of day-to-day living.

That new pattern for your life begins as you make the effort to include your parents along with other important people in your daily schedule. How often will you visit them? Do you want a regular schedule? Would your parents prefer to know when you will come to see them, so they have something to look forward to? Or would they prefer a surprise? Will you see them on weekdays for a brief time or wait until weekends when you can spend more time with them?

I stopped by to see Dad at the nursing home each evening on my way home from work. It became a part of his routine and mine. My family at home became adjusted to the fact that I got home half an hour later than before. To them it seemed that I worked a little longer—except that I had stories about Grandpa. Since the home served dinner earlier than we did at home, I was with my father for his dinner. He liked that and ate better. Others in my family went by to see him now and then, but he could count on me at a regular time, five days a week.

If your parents have come to live with you, the above process is reversed. You plan for the time when you will be away from home. You will still need to do shopping, visit friends, take part in civic and social activities, as well as give attention to your job and family. You need to establish that routine from the very beginning so that it becomes a part of the way things go with your parents in your home.

My biggest problem when my mother came to live with me was that I felt I lost control of all my personal time. She slipped back into the old habit of asking me what time I would be back each time I left the house. I wasn't used to that anymore. My friends couldn't drop by for a visit with me as they had before, because my mother was a part of the conversation. She was so glad to have company that she forgot that they had come to see me, and she took over the visit.

Such problems must be recognized and dealt with during the adjustment time. Once routines have been established they are hard to change.

You may need to tell your parents that you are expecting company and that you would appreciate it if they would watch TV in their room. If it works, you can take the risk of having them join you for refreshments later in the evening. You will also need to recognize that all family members like to know when others are coming home. Some people worry about car accidents every time someone is away. Show normal consideration to your parents, but do not return to the status of a child living with parents.

Help your parents also see that life goes on for them. Too often elderly people regard a move to live with their children or into a care facility as the end of their normal life. Help them to see that it is not true. Help them take things with them that will make them feel at home where they live. Give them choices about clothes. Talk about how you will celebrate birthdays, anniversaries, Christmas, and other holidays.

Before Aunt Emma moved into a nursing home, she divided most of her personal belongs up among her family and friends. She thought she wouldn't need any of them anymore. However, after a few weeks in the nursing home she realized that life was going on. She asked for all of her things to be returned. It caused a little upset in the family, but it was good for Aunt Emma.

The following story, which I read long ago in *Reader's Digest,* has helped me understand the adjustment to nursing home living. When my 85-year-old mother went to a nursing home, she took a small suitcase, perhaps to show that she didn't intend to stay very long. I had only been home a short time after dropping her off when she phoned. "Bring me a couple of my good dresses from the closet and a better pair of shoes," she said. "There are *men* in this place."

If your family is like most others, you have stories about the things that have happened over the years. The history of your parents will not stop now. Their move into your home or to another type of home will add more stories. Their history will continue to grow.

How Do You Stay Involved?

If the decision has been for your parents to live with you—or you with them—you will have no problem about how you will be involved in their lives. In that case, your concern will be how to stay involved in other important parts of your life. The following list will help to make you aware of some possible conflicts.

1. Cooking, eating, and cleaning up. Mealtime is an important part of family life, and it can be a source of joy. But conflicts can also arise in the kitchen. Sometimes the parents may see themselves as guests to be served. At other times they may want to take over the kitchen. Either idea can cause problems. Establish the ground rules about who cooks, when meals are served, and who cleans up.

> Our biggest problem about having my husband's mother live in our home was that she could not stay out of the kitchen. I suppose it sounds as though I should have been glad to have someone help with the cooking and cleaning. But it didn't work that way. She would forget and leave burners on. We are lucky that she did no more harm than ruin a couple of pans. She dropped good silverware in the garbage disposal. I couldn't scold her like a child, but I couldn't let her harm herself and others either.

When you and your parents live together you may lose the special event of having them to your home for a special meal. That can be solved by still having a special dinner once a week or month; it is a time when they become guests again. If their health permits, a dinner out once in a while will serve the same purpose. They may even want to treat you by picking up the tab.

2. Getting mail and receiving phone calls are another important part of home routine. Who goes to get the mail? Does anyone feel an invasion of privacy? Is there a danger that letters or messages might be lost?

> I have a friend whose mother moved into their home. The friend's husband operated his business from the home. The arrangement did not last because the mother would

get the mail and answer the phone. Her son-in-law accused her of ruining his business and made a rule that she could not touch the phone or go to the mailbox. She soon moved out.

Another family found a solution:

> When my mother moved in with us we agreed that she would have her own phone. Fortunately, she was even able to keep the same number she had had before. It cost a little extra each month, but it was worth it for the privacy both she and my family had. The phone was also a good symbol for Mom that she still had her own life.

Other simple arrangements can be made. Whoever reads the newspaper first should fold it up and put it in a designated area. The TV guide stays in a certain place. These may sound like small issues, but family tensions are caused by a collection of small—even laughable—events that build up to cause the family version of a major earthquake.

3. People living in the same home need to respect each others' privacy and schedule. Family members who go to work or school get dibs on the bathroom during rush hour in the morning. Those who get up early or stay up late need to be aware of others who require their sleep.

Everyone involved needs to understand that the arrangement in your home will require each family member to make some adjustments for the sake of others. The best way is to talk about expectations and to build into your system a way of checking to see how it is working. One way to do this it to ask all who live in the house to pretend that they are writing a TV sitcom about a family like your own. What would be the problems on the television episode? What would be funny? How would the characters resolve their situation? All TV programs have to find solutions within thirty or sixty min-

9 • Living With Your Decision

utes, with time out for commercials. Allow yourselves more time than that, and feel free to take "commercial breaks" when the mood warrants.

Now consider your continued involvement with your parents if they move to some kind of home for the elderly. How will you still be involved in their lives? Their biggest fear is that they will be abandoned by their family. From their point of view you (or they) are paying someone to do what family should do.

First, don't make promises that you cannot keep. You need to establish how often you will visit your parents, how long you will stay, and what you will do. That third part—what you will do—will give meaning to your visits.

In some cases the visits between the residents of a home and their family cause tensions for both. For example, if you go because you feel it is your duty, and that others will criticize you if you don't visit your parents, you are starting with a problem. You will not enjoy the visit, and your parents will know it. You need to work out ways so the visit is for your good as well as the good of your parents.

For your parents, a visit by a child or grandchild is the highlight of the day or week. It is important to them as people, but it is also important for their status among other residents and the staff. Being able to say "My daughter visited me today" gives the same sense of achievement in a nursing home as "I bowled a 250 game last night" or "I bought a new car" does in the workplace. But the truth is that visits to an elderly person in a nursing home can be difficult. The old person's mental and physical health may make it hard to have a conversation.

I dreaded to visit my dad in the nursing home. He was in pain all the time; I could see it. The medication made his mind wander. He would hold my hand to keep me there. And I would wish that he would die. He's been dead for five years and I still feel guilty that I wished him dead. I can't forget how I felt as I sat in that room.

Do not avoid your parents because they are in physical pain or have lost mental abilities. They need you all the more. Before I visit people who have those kind of problems I remind myself that they have the pain whether I am there or not. If I avoid the visit, I may avoid knowing about the pain. But if I visit them, they have a distraction from their pain. Those who study such things say that a visitor can reduce a patient's pain by five percent. That makes sense because the visitor shares that much of the pain. But for a loved one, even five percent is a good deal. And I am glad to feel five percent of someone's pain if I know that the other person has a little relief because of my visit.

> My Aunt Frieda was generally tense and nervous when I visited her in the nursing home. I would watch her calm down a little bit as we visited. It was one of the things that made it worthwhile for me to take the time to go see her.

If your parents lose their mental abilities, you need to accept the problem and not make them feel guilty about their condition. Sometimes they are aware of their loss.

> Anna is a special joy to me. One day she said, "I know something is going wrong in my mind. I can't understand it." I asked, "Does your mind take a little vacation now and then?"
>
> "No," she answered. "It's more than that."
>
> "Is your mind retired?" I asked.
>
> "Yes, that's it," she replied. We had a good laugh about it. When I walked out of her room I prayed that if my mind retires I can accept it as gracefully as Anna did.

9 • Living With Your Decision

The second and more difficult reason that some visits to parents in a home is a problem is that there has always been a strained relationship between parent and child.

> I dreaded my weekly visit with Mom in the nursing home. She would always be sweet and nice to other visitors—especially the pastor. But when we were alone she would complain about everything. She had a long list of my failures that went back to my childhood. She would repeat them over and over, and I could not defend myself. She made me relive problems that I had worked out in my own life since I had married. She set me back years in my personal life.

Perhaps that person's experience is extreme, but it is not unusual. If you have a difficult relationship with your parents and your visits to them upset you, recognize that it also upsets them. It is not good for you or for them to let them beat you up psychologically. From their point of view, you may be doing the same thing to them.

Talk about the problem with your parents. Tell them that you want to see them, but that you cannot handle the criticism or the complaining. Put restrictions on the subjects discussed. If they violate the rules, remind them of the agreement and leave. Come back as soon as you can to give them another chance. If you let the complaining and criticizing continue, you are becoming an accessory to their problem. You are allowing them to make themselves and others—including you—miserable.

If this remains a problem for you, seek professional counseling. It also may help to get acquainted with the children of other residents in the home where your parents live. Often sharing experiences with others increases your understanding. Maybe you can even team up and visit your parents together. Then your parents will have to be on their good behavior because they have company.

You must acknowledge and deal with any problem that makes your visits to your parents difficult. The problem may be that you have not accepted your parents' physical and emotional limitations. Neither you nor they can live in the past. Accept their present needs and your present relationships. Bypass the problems and look for ways to have good visits.

If your parents behave better when people other than family members are present, take others along with you. Arrange to pick up some of their old friends or other relatives to go with you on the visit. Time your visits to coincide with others'.

Take something to do with you on the visit. In some cases the elderly do not have the energy or ability for long conversations, but they want you to be with them. Take along hand work, a book, crossword puzzles. Tell your family member, "I want to sit with you for a while today. We don't have to talk. I'm here."

Better yet, if their health permits take along something that you can do together. Pictures of family members, and clippings from newspapers and magazines may give you something to talk about together. Bring large colorful pictures that you can put on the wall, if the home allows. Or bring drawings done by children.

Provide clothing for your parents that makes them feel good about themselves. Would your father occasionally like to dress up with a necktie? It might make him feel that he was back on the job again— or getting ready for a big event. Your mother might like certain jewelry or flowers to wear.

Alvenia always has brightly colored dresses and inexpensive but attractive jewelry. It gives me something to say as I compliment her appearance, and she will point out how the earrings match a certain color in her dress. It makes her feel good to look nice.

9 • Living With Your Decision

Also bring along things that your parents might have from their earlier lives but can't keep in their new home. Take an old family picture album one time. Wedding pictures another. Maybe they have awards or souvenirs stored away somewhere. Dig them out and let them see those things again.

Bring a tape recorder with music, or interviews with family members from a gathering of the clan. With an awareness of diet restrictions, bring things to eat. Remember that people like good smells. Take a warm cookie or piece of homemade bread. Take flowers that they can touch and smell. Give them a pot-pourri or sachet— first for them to enjoy and then for them to have something to give to a favorite nurse or other staff person.

Take along Christmas cards and other greetings that you receive. Leave some with them. Provide decorations for special occasions such as Halloween, Thanksgiving, and Valentine's Day.

Even if you are unable to visit your parents regularly, send them cards and notes in the mail. Everyone likes to have a letter to open. Again , mail is often a status symbol for them. A letter to a person in a home for the elderly shows that someone cares. If you have to be away for a while, plan to send cards, have a gift delivered, or ask someone else to fill in for you in your regular visiting hours.

All of these ideas are thought starters. The concept is this: Do something to make both you and your parents enjoy your visits. Create something to talk about and to do.

Other Social Contacts

It is important that you do not become the only contact between your parents and the rest of the world. You can encourage others to visit your parents by telling them where your parents are, the best time to visit, and other details to make the visit easy.

Make a list of those people who are important in your

parents' lives. Some of them could visit on a regular basis. Others could drop by while you are on vacation or for a special season. Others could make phone calls or send cards.

When you mail out your Christmas cards to friends and family who also know your parents, include their address and suggest that others remember your parents. You might also include a reminder to others about your parents' birthdays, wedding anniversary and the like so the attention is not limited to one holiday season.

For ease of writing, I have been referring to your parents in the plural. In some cases it is true that a husband and wife grow old together and remain husband and wife together as they go through steps of assisted living homes to nursing homes. But in most cases it will be one person alone.

Intimacy and sexuality are important for all human beings. It may be difficult for you to discuss this issue because of two taboos. First we are talking about your parents. Most parents and children developed a system long ago in which each generation says to the other, "We won't think about your sex life and we don't want you to think about ours."

The second taboo is that we are talking about old people. "Old" means anyone at least a decade older than ourselves—and, from our point of view, old people aren't interested in intimacy or sex. I'm not here to argue the point, but trust me on this one: It's certainly not true for all old people. As I gathered material for this book our local paper carried a syndicated question-and-answer column that included this question: "Do you know of a nursing home that permits open affection and lovemaking among the residents?"

Those who work in nursing homes have many stories that often border on voyeurism about the sexual interest and activities of residents. Let's deal with it not as an invasion of privacy but as an understanding of people's need for contact with others—and that does not always mean it has to be sexual intercourse. But it does mean that elderly people still enjoy the company of people of the opposite sex, that they need to touch and to be touched, and in many cases they at least want to think about sexual activity.

For married couples who are well established in their relationship, they can often be in a nursing home and continue to be husband and wife in the same way that they had been before. They have grown together and understand each other's sexual needs.

However a nursing home romance rarely develops into a bonded, lasting relationship with or without marriage. My congregation has a weekly nursing-home ministry. Residents who attend often regard me as their pastor even though they don't belong to my congregation or denomination. One man and woman asked me to marry them. Through the management of the home I found that each had children and all were against a marriage, as was the nursing home. I talked to the couple and realized they needed each other as special friends. They continued to come to worship together, to eat together and watch TV together, but marriage was forgotten with no problem.

My experience has been, and it was verified by the answer to the questions mentioned above, that men and women need contact with each other in nursing homes. One elderly member of my parish was in a depression after the death of his wife. Six months later he was assigned a dinner table with three elderly women in a nursing home. He referred to them as "the girls." He became more alert. They all enjoyed the dinner conversation. It was the kind of intimacy that both he and the women needed. When he was hospitalized at one time, he was eager to get back to the nursing home so he wouldn't lose his place at their table.

Do not be alarmed by the stories you may have heard about seductions in the nursing homes. It certainly has happened, but it is not limited to nursing homes. More important is that you recognize that your mother or father may enjoy being in the presence of someone of the opposite sex for conversation and perhaps some hand holding. They are not being unfaithful to your other parent. They are being normal.

You need to encourage your parents to make friends in the place where they live. Most facilities for the elderly offer social activities. Encourage and help your parents participate in such activities. Look for people who came from the same area of the country, did the same kind of work, belong to the same church, went to the same college, or share other experiences that bring people together. Don't be jealous if you come to visit your parents and find they are busy with friends. That's the way it should be.

The employees of the home where your parents will live also will be an important social contact for both you and your parents. You have already noticed that in my opinion the staff is the most important part of any home for the elderly. You may have heard stories about cruelty of nursing home employees to the residents. You may have heard about those who steal the patients' possessions and eat their food. I have no doubt that some of those stories could be true. In any occupation (including mine and yours) there are people who are cruel, dishonest, and who are using their position to hurt others. But in my experience the vast majority of employees in facilities for elderly people are hard working and caring people. You can help your parents by showing an interest in and an appreciation for the nursing home staff.

You need to watch both your own attitude and that of your parents as you develop your relationship with the employees of the place you have selected for your parents. Take the time to get acquainted with those who will have daily contact with your parents. If your parents have a difficult name, help the staff people learn how to pronounce it. (My family name scares many when they first look at it. It is spelled WE IS HE IT and pronounced "WHY-SITE.") If your parents have strong opinions about being called Mr. or Mrs., or if they like or dislike normal nicknames associated with their given names, let staff people know by putting a name tag on your parents when they first arrive. This little detail helps staff people see something special to remember in your parents. That is especially necessary in a large home with many different shifts of workers. Also help your parents learn the names of the people from the home with whom they have the most contact. Speak the name often to your parents. You may even want to make a list of the names of people for your parents.

Show your appreciate to any staff person who gives special attention to your parents. Do not ask for special favors that are not offered, but accept the loving care that some nursing-home employees offer. Many people work in homes for the elderly because they truly love old people and want to make their lives worthwhile. Find those people and encourage them. Everyone appreciates a "Thank you" for a job well done.

I was surprised when I visited my mother in a board and care home and found her upset. She had been there for over a year and was always happy about the home. On this visit she found fault with the food, the noise, and everything else. Finally she told me that the woman in charge of the day shift had retired, "just left us" in Mother's words. Mom was angry that her friend had retired—"She's only sixty-two years old and as strong as an ox." I had to recognize that my mother's reaction was a normal feeling for one who had lost a friend. I was even glad to know that she had become so attached to an employee of the home, and I tried to get her to share my view.

If your parents develop a personality conflict with a staff member, understand that not every staff person can relate well to every resident. Help your parents find out what the problem is. Do not let it become a daily source of irritation.

You can help your parents make friends with other residents in a home. Look for people who share the same interests and have the same level of communication skills as your parents. Bring things to your parents that they could share with other residents. Include others in a discussion or a game.

> I went to visit Dad two days after he had moved into a board and care home. He was in his private room and had his radio on. I asked him if he had met any of his new neighbors yet. "No," he said, "but there is a guy out there named Art who sits and stares at the TV all day. I figure I'll get him to talk to me one way or the other." I knew Dad would adjust to his new home.

What About Their Spiritual Life?
By now you know that I am a pastor and that I think faith is an important part of life. But this book is about your parents' needs—and yours. So with the understanding of my point of view, let's look at yours.

Do you and your parents share the same religious convictions? That means not only do you belong to the same religious denomination and perhaps the same congregation, but does your faith have the same priority? If you have the same point of view, you can easily deal with these issues together—either by thinking that they are unnecessary or by working together to continue your parents' spiritual life in their new surroundings.

However, if you and your parents have different views on religion you need to be aware of those differences and not let them cause stress in your relationship. Let's look at three possibilities.

1. Suppose that you have a deep spiritual life and your

9 • Living With Your Decision

parents have none. They think they don't need religion. In that case, you may want to share your faith with them. Since you are now making decisions for them—just as they made decisions for you when you were young—you may use your authority to push your faith. This is a proper thing for you to do *if* your parents can accept the spiritual ministry you are offering. They may appreciate it and recognize that you are showing your love for them by sharing your faith. But they may resent it and think that you are trying to use their limitations against them. You cannot share a religion of love by force or manipulation. Remember, your goal is to have a spiritual bond with your parents. Do not let your concern have a reverse effect. You might be wise to let a third person speak of faith to your parents, if you have reason to believe that they would resent you for doing it.

2. Suppose your parents have a strong faith, but spirituality is not important to you. You must be concerned for their needs. Do not use your position of power to prevent them from having contact with those who share their faith. Find out what they need for their spiritual life and look for others to provide that need if you cannot do it.

3. Another possibility is that you and your parents have different religious convictions. Do not let these differences cause a tug-of- war between you. Find out what you do share in common. Perhaps you are both Christian, but belong to different denominations. Find the things common in your Christian faith and use them to bridge the areas of difference.

Your situation may be complicated by other religious views held by other members of the family. But the point is that for many people faith is a vital part of life. Some people who have ignored God all of their lives will get interested in him if they think they are going to spend eternity with him. Others who have been very active in church all of their lives will lose interest as they grow older.

It is important, though, that they not feel rejected or forgotten by their church.

> Lillian's one big complaint about the nursing home was that she could not be involved in church work. She missed working on crafts for the bazaar. She missed cooking church dinners and being on the altar guild. She didn't like to have visitors from the church because they only reminded her of what she was missing. Her complaints gave me an opportunity to appreciate the work she had done for church, but also to remind her of why she did those things. As we came to talk about her service to Christ, she saw what she had done in a new light. As she remembered the joy it gave her when she did church work, she saw she had a new opportunity—that is, to let others help her now so they could enjoy it. That gave her a mission in life. She had served others; now she could be served.

One of the most frustrating parts of my visiting members of my congregation who live in homes for the elderly is that every other resident also would like for me to stop for a visit. I have had to deal with the fact that I cannot become a full-time chaplain to homes for the aged; yet I see a great need for spiritual care for the elderly.

As I visited one member in the day room of a board and care home, another elderly person said (very loudly), "I wish I had a pastor who would visit me." Her words echoed in my ears as I had to drive on to other calls. I realized that she could have meant two things.

She may have meant that she had a pastor, but that the pastor did not have the time or the desire to come to see her. That view of her statement made me more aware of the need for me to call on people in homes. It also made me aware of how important it is that our congregation does not depend on me alone to call on elderly people. We have weekly worship services in two nursing homes. We have elders and Stephen Ministers who also make calls in other homes. If you are a church member, you need to see your congregation as a resource to help you serve your parents. You may be able to enlist other individuals, staff members and boards in your congregation to put together Jesus' instructions to love God and our neighbors by establishing or increasing a ministry to the elderly.

> When I started volunteering for our congregation's nurs-
> ing- home ministry, I hated it. I remembered my own par-
> ents, who are now dead. I saw myself as the little old man
> in a wheelchair. I thought the people were dull and dirty.
> But I kept going. Now I enjoy being in the nursing home.
> Those people need me. I need them.

Back to the woman who said that she wished she had a pastor to call on her. The other meaning of her statement could be that she may not have had a pastor because she did not belong to a church. In a previous chapter we discussed the "more so" theory of old age. It says that as people age they stay the way they always have been except they become "more so." If they were pleasant, easygoing people in their earlier years they will become more so as they grow older. If they were grouches all of their lives, they will become grouchier as they grow older.

I don't believe the "more so" theory is always true but I think it does apply to faith. People who have included worship, prayer, and Bible reading in their lives will feel a need for those things as they grow older. I have seen family members become embarrassed when parents or grandparents say no to an offer for prayer or Bible reading. But I understand. What held no interest before, still holds no interest.

Aging Parents

On the other hand, those who have included religious activities as an important part of their lives will need them even more when they are in a home for the elderly. They should be taken to worship services and activities in their church for as long as possible. When they can no longer go to public worship, they need worship to come to them. Some homes have regular worship services offered by a variety of denominations in the community. Some churches have activities in the homes for the elderly only at Christmas and Easter, while others offer a monthly service. A weekly worship service and/or Bible study is better because that is what fits the previous pattern. The need that your parents feel for worship services may influence which home you select for them.

If the home where your parents will live does not have regular worship services, check what is available. Some places, especially assisted-living homes, will offer transportation to church services. The families who operate small board and care homes will sometimes take residents to church. Your congregation might provide an audio or videotape of their worship service to be taken to members who are shut-ins. Such tapes would give your parents a sense of participation in their own church—and give you something to share with your parents in their new home.

Music is an important way for people to express their faith. The worship services that our congregation conducts in two nursing homes are clearly offered to all Christians; though they are listed on the facility's schedule under our denomination. We deliberately sing songs that would appeal to the memories of Christians who grew up in other denominations. We even have a few people who are not Christian but who come because they enjoy the music.

Many people also want to hear the Bible, either in a sermon or taught in a class. Maybe one of the reasons that I enjoy my nursing home ministry is that it is the only place

9 • Living With Your Decision

that I ever get a complaint that the sermon is too short. Those who attend church in the nursing home are not going shopping, dining, or golfing after worship. In addition, I have seen many people who do not appear to be tuned in to reality perk up when they here a favorite Bible story or verse. I am convinced that those who have lost a lot of mental ability can still focus on a message that they have heard from childhood.

Praying is also an important part of worship. When people pray together they acknowledge their relationship with one another and with God. When people give prayer requests, I often realize that they have been able to hear and understand more than I had counted on. Often even those who seem totally unaware of what is happening will respond when they hear the Lord's Prayer. I often see lips move and sometimes hear low voices join in the prayer.

My favorite name for the Lord's Supper or Eucharist is "Communion"; I believe it gives a communion with God and with one another. When I give the bread and wine to an individual or a small group in a home for the elderly, I do three things. First, I establish the human communion by talking with the person or people. If they are from my congregation I try to bring them up to date on what is happening in the parish. I want them to be aware of the community to which they still belong. Then I use a form of worship that they are used to. I depend on their previous experience to understand what is happening. Finally, we share in the Lord's Supper.

Mom doesn't remember much anymore. Often she forgets my name. She will tell me that no one has come to visit her for a month, when I know my children saw her two days before. But when the pastor comes, he shows her the little kit he carries for the Lord's Supper. She watches him get out the bread and the little glass. She has received

Holy Communion all of her life and it seems to bring her mind back on track.

One more experience from my own ministry that I want to share with you in your situation. I have had a number of elderly members in nursing homes who were members of my congregation, but whose family did not share their faith. When the elderly person died there was no funeral or memorial at our church because the family felt no need. I also have had many active members who had elderly members who had no need for church and did not want a pastor or church member to call on them. Yet when the elderly person died, the family needed a funeral for their sake. You can see the odd reversal here. I tell you this because I think you should apply it to your situation. Talk to your pastor or your parents' pastor now. Make plans now so a funeral can be held to serve the purpose it offers.

You Have Done More Than Make a Decision
You have worked hard to provide the best place possible for your parents. All of your efforts have done more than make the choice for your parents' care. In order to make that decision you have had to establish a number of patterns that will be helpful to you and your parents on other issues.

You have recognized and accepted the new relationship between you and your parents in which you have become responsible for part of, if not all of, the decisions in their lives. You have discovered how members of your family can (or cannot) work together to provide for your parents. You have learned how your parents will accept (or not accept) the help you offer them. By learning these things you have also learned what advantages and disadvantages you'll have as you continue to help your parents.

Finding the place for your parents to live in their old age probably was not the first, and probably will not be the last, decision that you need to make for them. Because finding a place for them to live was a major decision involving not only other people but also requiring you to evaluate financial and community resources, you are now better equipped to make other decisions for your parents.

Do your parents have special legal needs regarding business, investments, taxes, trusts, wills etc.? Many communities now have lawyers with a specialty in elder law. Why not go ahead and take care of those issues now while you and your family are focused on your parents need?

Do you know how your parents and other members of your family feel about life-support systems? Would your parents want to be kept alive by such systems? Do they want to sign a living will? Does your state also require a durable power of attorney for such decisions?

Do your parents have strong feelings about embalming, cremation, where they are to be buried? Who will make those decisions for them, if they have not made their wishes known?

These and other issues are beyond the scope of this book. However, they are a part of the care that you need to provide for your parents. By establishing communication within your family and by accepting responsibilities, you are making it easier for all of you to deal with such decisions.

This final story is mine. When I first became a pastor over thirty years ago I did not enjoy working with elderly people. It was a duty that I had to do. I often felt it took too much of my time, and I wondered if it was of any value. I even expressed my discontent in print in a book entitled *Excuse Me, Sir (Excerpts from a Man's Conversation with God)* (Concordia Publishing House).

Aging Parents

Southhaven Nursing Home

They come by wheel chair,
    by walker,
    by short halting steps such as
    they used to begin their
    walk through life and now
    again as they end it.
Their faces are grooved phonograph records.
The eye of youth travels alaong the wrinkles
    to feel the sorrow,
        love, hate,
         fear, futility,
        hope, joy,
        pain
    that have been impressed
        on the record of a life.
Broad gold rings ride loose on bony, blue fingers,
Evidence that this body was once desired
    and claimed by a man.
Bodies that gave life
    now dwindle away like old seed pods.
We call it the golden' years
    in a nursing home.
But is it really
    post-life in a pre-mausoleum?

But many old people taught me many lessons. I learned to
listen to them before I talked to them. They shared a view of
life that I had not seen before. Now that I am nearing retirement I have an opportunity to write this book about being
with old people. I hope that I have passed on to you what
many old people, and those who love them, have taught me.
If I live to be old and need to be in a nursing home, I will be
glad that one is available. I will go into that home with a
strong resolution to make the people who live there and the
people who work there be glad that I am also there.

——Appendix 1——
Questionnaire Regarding
Housing for the Elderly

This questionnaire can be a useful resource for those who must make decisions for their aging parents. You may apply these questions to others such as spouse, grandparents, other relatives, friend, etc.

1. How are you preparing for the time when your parents will not be able to live alone?
2. What plans have your parents made for the time when they will not be able to live alone?
3. How will your family choose the person(s) to make the decisions regarding your parents living arrangements?
4. (For the decision maker) What other parts of your life (other family members, employment, living situation) will affect the decision regarding your parents?
5. What are your immediate options concerning a place for

your parents to live? Have any been automatically rejected? Why? What options have you not even considered?

6. What financial considerations are important in your
decision?
7. What medical considerations are important in your
decision?
8. What geographical considerations are important in your
decision?
9. What spiritual considerations are important in your
decision?
10. Is it good to think of a decision regarding where your
parents are to live as permanent or as temporary? Why?
11. What things do you think will make the change easier
for your parents?
12. How will the experience of making plans for your parents draw you closer to them, or cause difficulties
between you and them? Explain.
13. How might the decision regarding your parents bring
you closer to other members of the family or cause tension in the family? Explain.
14. From your experience what would you tell others to
help them as they go through the same experience?

For parents who want to assist in decisions regarding their living arrangements

1. Have you written or discussed your preferences in the
event you can no long live alone or with your family?
2. What has your family done that helped you? What have
they done that you did not like?
3. Whom do you want to make decisions for you in case
you are not able to make them for yourself? Does the rest
of our family know about your choice?

Appendix 1

For caregivers in homes or agencies that provide for aged people:

1. How have you helped (or could you help) the families of those who can no longer live alone?
2. What are the good things you have seen families do for the elderly? What problems have you seen?
3. What are the advantages of the type of care your facility gives?
4. Would some people who have chosen to live in your facility be better off in a different type of agency?

——Appendix 2——
Residents' Rights in a Board and Care Home

YOU HAVE THE RIGHT...

... to receive courteous, fair, and respectful care and treatment with full recognition of your dignity and individuality.

... to exercise your civil and religious liberties, including the right to make personal decisions and to rely on the home's staff in exercising these liberties.

... to communicate, associate, and meet privately with your friends, relatives, physician, attorney, or any other persons of your choice.

... to access a telephone to make and receive calls and to send and receive any correspondence without interception or interference by the staff.

... to manage your own financial affairs or to have them administered by an authorized person outside the facility. The home does not handle the personal business matters of its residents.

... to be free from physical, emotional, mental and chemical abuse, physical restraints, and the use of psychoactive drugs for purpose of discipline or convenience.

... to have your personal, financial, and health records kept in confidence.

... to receive a written statement of the customary services that the home will provide you and any additional services that will be provided if you need them. Your Admission Agreement must include a written statement of all your monthly fees and expenses. No fees in excess of those stated in your Admission Agreement can be charged to you without your approval, unless you are advised 30 days in advance or if the additional fee charged is to cover emergency services.

... to a written statement from the home 30 days prior to transfer or termination of your Admission Agreement.

... to present grievances on behalf of yourself and others. These may be presented, without fear of reprisal, to the home's staff or to any other person.

... to join with others within or outside the home to work for improvements in care.

... to have privacy in treatment and care for personal needs including your intimate personal hygiene.

Appendix 2

... to keep possessions as space allows and to be assured of security for any other personal possessions stored by the home.

... to a statement of the rules of the home and an explanation of your responsibility to obey all reasonable rules.

——Appendix 3——
Residents' Admission Agreement

(The document is provided by the federal government and must be signed by all residents or their legal guardians as they enter a nursing home facility.)

1. The Resident has the right to be treated with consideration, respect, and full recognition of his or her dignity and individuality.

2. The Resident has the right to be free from mental or physical abuse, corporal punishment, involuntary seclusion, and any physical or chemical restraints imposed for purposes other than treating medical symptoms. Restraints may only be imposed on the Resident to ensure the physical safety of Resident or other residents and only upon the written order of a physician.

3. The Resident has the right to organize and participate in resident groups in the Nursing Center, and have members of the Resident's family meet in the Nursing Center with the families of other residents.

4. The Resident has the right to privacy with regard to his or her agreed upon accommodations, medical treatment, written and telephone communications, visits, meetings of family, and meetings of resident groups at the Nursing Center.

5. The Resident has the right to participate in social, religious and community activities that do not interfere with the rights of other residents in the Nursing Center.

6. The Resident shall be encouraged and assisted throughout his or her stay in the Center to exercise the rights defined in this document as well as those entitled to the Resident as a U.S. citizen.

7. The Resident has the right to manage his or her own personal financial affairs or have a Legal Representative handle those affairs on behalf of the Resident.

8. The Resident has the right to voice grievances regarding treatment or care that is discriminatory or retaliatory.

9. The Resident has the right to recommend changes in Nursing Center policies and services to the Center's staff and/or to outside representatives without fear or restraint, interference, coercion, discrimination, or reprisal.

10. The Resident has the right to file a complaint with the appropriate state agency concerning resident abuse or neglect as well as misappropriation of resident property in the Nursing Center.

Appendix 3

11. The Resident has the right to be visited by any representative of the U.S. Department of Health and Human Services, representatives of the state or the state's long care ombudsperson, the Resident's physician, family or relatives, or any group of people who provide health, social, legal or other services to the resident. These visits are subject to the reasonable and appropriate rules and regulations of the Nursing Center.

12. The Resident has the right to examine, with reasonable notice, the results of the Nursing Center's most recent survey conducted by representatives of the Department of Health and Human Services and the plan of correction prepared by the Nursing Center in response to the survey.

13. The Resident has the right to choose a personal attending physician, be fully informed in advance about care and treatment, and participate in planning medical treatment.

14. The Resident has the right to contract with the providers of his or her choice, including a pharmacy, unless prohibited by the applicable law, as long as the providers agree to and follow the reasonable rules and regulations of the Nursing Center.

15. The Resident has the right to be fully informed by the attending physician of his or her medical condition unless medically contraindicated.

16. The Nursing Center's qualified nursing staff may administer psychopharmocologic drugs to the Resident, only on the order of the physician and only as a part of a written plan of care that is designed to eliminate or modify the symptoms for which the drugs are prescribed. In addition, this plan of care must be periodically reviewed by an

independent consultant as required by law.

17. The Resident has the right to refuse medical treatment or medication, as allowed by the applicable law.

18. The Resident has the right to refuse participation in programs that are not included in the written plan of care.

19. The Resident has the right to refuse participating in scientific research.

20. The Resident's personal and clinical medical records will be treated confidentially as required by the applicable law.

21. The Resident may review his or her medical record upon written request to the facility, 24 hours in advance.

22. The Resident has the right to be admitted to the Nursing Center and convert payment status to Medicaid without regard to race, color, sex, age, nationality, or handicap.

23. The Resident has the right to reside in the Nursing Center and receive services with reasonable accommodation of his or her individual needs and preferences, except where the health or safety of the Resident or other residents would be endangered.

24. The Resident has the right to keep and use personal clothing and possessions in the Nursing Center as space permits unless doing so would infringe upon the rights and safety of other residents, or unless medically contraindicated by the Resident's physician.

25. The Resident has the right to privacy during spousal visits.

Appendix 3

26. The Resident may occupy the same room as his or her spouse if the spouse is also a resident of the Nursing Center and agrees to the cohabitation, unless medically contraindicated by either the Resident's physician or documentation in the medical record.

27. The Resident has the right to have access to a telephone while in the Nursing Center.

28. The Resident has the right to receive appropriate advance notice of any involuntary transfer within or discharge from the Nursing Center, as required by the appropriate law.

29. The Resident has the right to receive notice before his or her roommate is changed by the Center.

30. The Resident has the right to refuse to be transferred or discharged from the Nursing Center unless one of the following are true:

    a. The transfer or discharge is necessary for the Resident's health and welfare because these needs cannot be met in the current Nursing Center.

    b. The Resident's health has improved sufficiently to a point where the services of the Nursing Center are no longer necessary.

    c. The health, welfare, or safety of employees or residents in the Nursing Center are endangered by the Resident's continued stay.

    d. The Resident has failed, after reasonable and appropriate notice, to pay or arrange payment for charges incurred during his or her stay at the Nursing Center.

e. The Nursing Center ceases to operate and/or is no longer authorized to care for the Resident under applicable law.

31. The Nursing Center will inform the Resident, verbally and in writing at the time of admission, of the Resident's rights during his or her stay in the Nursing Center, in a language that the resident understands. In addition, the Center will notify the Resident of any changes made to these rights.

32. The Resident has the right to refuse a room transfer if the purpose of the transfer is to move the Resident to a Medicare- certified bed in order to obtain Medicare coverage for his/her stay.

33. The Resident has the right to have access to his/her current medical record, upon request to the Nursing Center within 24 hours (excluding weekends or holidays).

34. The Resident has the right to Nursing Center compliance with the terms of a signed written directive concerning medical care (e.g. Durable Power of Attorney, living wills, etc.) that complies with applicable state law.

—Appendix 4—
Where to Get
Help Fast

This book has suggested many people and agencies who can help you in your decision regarding care for your elderly parents. Below is a short recap of those who may be able to give you the information that will help you in your situation.

1. Those who know people who are in care facilities for the elderly because they work with elderly people.

   a. Physicians and counselors—especially those whose primary practice is with elderly people or with families.

   b. Church workers—especially those who work through congregations that have a Senior Citizen and/or Family Ministry program.

213

   c. Friends and coworkers who have members of their family in homes for the elderly.

2. The Yellow Pages. Look under:
   a. Nursing Homes
   b. Retirement Homes
   c. Boarding Homes (with special care for the elderly)
   d. Convalescent Home

Under the above general listings you will also find Associations, Organizations and Referral Services that represent a greater number of possible facilities, many of them often smaller and perhaps less-expensive places.

3. Government agencies (Look in the phone book under City, County, State and Federal government listings. Often the offices of government agencies are listed in a separate "Blue Pages" section.):

   a. Public Housing Management
   b. Senior Citizen Centers
   c. Public Health Nursing
   d. Medicare/Medicaid
   e. Home Health Services
   f. Public Fiduciary
   g. Council on Aging
   h. Blind Services
   i. Hearing Impaired Services
   j. Talking Books
   k. Social Security Adminisration (1-800-722-1213)

4. American Association of Retired Persons, 1909 K Street, N.W., Washington, D.C. 20049.